Table of Contents

HEARING THE SILENCE

A Critical Look at God's Silence and Claims of Divine Communication

RANDY WHITE

Hearing the Silence

A Critical Look at God's Silence and Claims of Divine Communication

All Scriptures are quoted from the King James Version.

ISBN: 978-1-961110-31-1

Library of Congress Cataloguing-in-Publication Data: LCCN: Pending

In order to get this book into publication as quickly as possible, we are using our Quick Print method. If you find errors, please email them to *editor@dispensationalpublishing.com* so that we can remove them in subsequent printings.

Dispensational Publishing House, Inc.

220 Paseo del Pueblo Norte

P.O. Box 3181

Taos, NM USA 87571

www.dispensationalpublishing.com

Ordering Information: Special discounts are available on quantity purchases by churches, associations, and U.S. trade bookstores and wholesalers. For details, contact the publisher at the address above or at our toll-free number: 1-844-321-4202.

Cover & interior layout by Ye Olde Typesetter, Show Low, AZ
Illustrations by Adobe Stock.
Author's photo on the Sea of Galilee by Shelley White

First Printing, December 2024
1 2 3 4 5 6 7 8 9 10 11 12

Introduction

As a pastor and theologian, I have long been concerned about the growing mysticism that has infiltrated both evangelical and fundamental churches. This trend, often cloaked in the language of spirituality and personal connection with God, has led to confusion, heartbreak, and spiritual disarray for countless believers. It has prompted me to write this book and host conferences addressing this critical issue.

One of the most poignant reminders of the damage this teaching can cause came in the form of a letter from a man named Nicholas. His story is one of many that inspired the urgency behind this work. Nicholas shared how his daughter, influenced by a ministry that emphasized hearing the "still small voice of God," was led into decisions that deeply fractured their family.

Despite his warnings and efforts to reason with her, his daughter believed she was following God's direct instructions. The consequences were devastating: strained relationships, unfulfilled obligations, and lingering questions about God's will in the face of tragedy. Nicholas's letter underscores the real-life implications of a misplaced trust in extra-biblical revelations.

He wrote, "I failed as a parent by not fully understanding [the ministry's] teachings. I thought their statement of faith was enough to ensure sound doctrine. I was wrong. With your teaching, I now have the tools to argue against these destructive ideas and properly divide the Word of

God. Thank you for all that you are doing. Your teaching may avert others from going through what I have experienced."

Nicholas's story is tragically not unique. Across the Christian world, believers are led to prioritize subjective impressions over the sufficiency of Scripture. Churches and ministries—often with the best of intentions—promote practices that leave individuals vulnerable to emotional manipulation, spiritual disappointment, and relational chaos.

In this book, I aim to expose the dangers of this mysticism, demonstrate the sufficiency of Scripture for every aspect of life, and call believers back to a faith grounded in the unchanging Word of God. My hope is that **Hearing the Silence** will equip you with biblical truth, helping you avoid the pitfalls of mysticism and find security in God's revealed Word. Let us commit ourselves to the authority of Scripture and resist the allure of voices God has never promised to give.

Randy White

Taos, NM

CHAPTER 1:

The Theology of Silence and the Sufficiency of Scripture

In a world where many believers seek to hear directly from God, it is vital to examine whether Scripture itself supports this expectation. This chapter explores the theology of divine silence, showing that God has already provided everything we need through His written Word. By walking through the sufficiency of Scripture, the biblical context of divine communication, and practical considerations, we invite you to embark on a journey that may free you from the mental turmoil and spiritual anguish of seeking what God has already fully given.

Faith, Hope, Love... and Silence? Are These Really All We Have?

Among many Christians today, there is a prevalent belief that God still speaks directly to individuals, offering personal guidance, insight, and instruction. This concept of hearing from God—whether through a "still small voice," an inner prompting, or other perceived divine communication—has become deeply ingrained in Christian practice. It is assumed by many that God continues to provide direct communication to believers, guiding them in daily decisions, spiritual growth, and life choices.

The belief is held so strongly that questioning this widely accepted belief often provokes strong opposition. Suggesting that God no longer speaks in such ways can result in accusations of heresy or disbelief in God's activity. Despite this, it is important to consider whether the Scriptures truly support the idea that God continues to offer personal revelation to each believer today. Upon close examination, many of the passages used to support modern-day divine communication were directed to Israel during the offer of the Kingdom (from Pentecost through A.D. 70), or even earlier, in the Gospels and the Old Testament. These texts do not directly apply to the church in the same way today.

The Perplexing Predicament of Modern Divine Communication

The challenge becomes evident when we compare the lives of believers who claim to hear from God with those who do not. If direct communication from God were an ongoing reality, we might expect Christians to live markedly different lives—protected from suffering, illness, poverty, and misfortune. Yet, the evidence suggests otherwise. Christians are no more immune to sorrow, sickness, evil, or financial instability than the general population.

Research shows that religious people, on average, live four years longer than those without religious faith, but this includes all forms of religion, not just Christianity. Moreover, Christians face the same natural disasters and personal hardships as non-believers. There is no clear evidence that those who claim to hear from God enjoy special divine favor or guidance that spares them from the difficulties of life.

This predicament forces us to reexamine the biblical texts. In 1 Corinthians 12:4-10, Paul describes a time when the Holy Spirit manifested visibly in the lives of believers. These manifestations of the Spirit, such as wisdom, knowledge, and miracles, were present in the early church and were unmistakable. However, this does not mean that such manifestations are still normative today. The spiritual gifts Paul refers to were for a specific time when God's plan for Israel and the church overlapped.

1 Corinthians 13:
The So-Called "Love Chapter"

Commonly known as the "love chapter," 1 Corinthians 13 actually speaks of the cessation of spiritual manifestations. Verses 8-10 indicate that these manifestations will cease. The question is not whether they will end, but when they have or will end. Here we find the key distinction between cessationists, who believe these gifts have already ceased, and continuationists, who believe they continue today. Cessationists must establish when the gifts ended, while continuationists must argue when they will cease in the future.

Paul offers a clue in verses 12-13, where he tells us that three things remain: *faith, hope, and charity*. Unlike the temporary spiritual manifestations, these three endure. However, even faith and hope are temporal, as they will no longer be needed in eternity. Love, on the other hand, remains the greatest because it transcends time. Today, Christians live by faith in the truth of Scripture, hope in the redemptive work of Christ, and love for God and others. The spiritual gifts that once confirmed and authenticated the message of the apostles have ceased, leaving us with these enduring qualities to guide us in our Christian walk.

Living in an Age of Silence

When Israel rejected her Messiah, God began transitioning into an age of silence. This silence is not new in history;

there was a similar period between the closing of the Old Testament and the arrival of Christ when God did not send new prophets or revelations. Yet, this period of silence does not suggest that God has lost His power or is uninvolved in the world.

An age of silence does not mean that God is incapable of performing miracles. Instead, it demonstrates His sovereignty and wisdom in working through natural means, rather than through direct, unmistakable acts of communication or intervention. Today, God works through His preserved Word and natural laws, not through new revelations or personal prophecies.

In this age of silence, God's work is carried out through His Word and His divine governance over the universe. He no longer provides new information because the full revelation of His will is complete in the Scriptures (1 Corinthians 13:8). There are no prophecies for this current age except for those concerning its conclusion in the rapture. Furthermore, angelic and demonic activity is restrained, and the spread of the gospel is entrusted to those who already know the truth. The responsibility lies with believers to share the message, not with divine intervention through visions or audible voices.

God's voice today is heard solely through the Scriptures. This age of silence affirms the sufficiency of His Word for every aspect of life and faith. Rather than expecting God to speak in new ways, believers are called to trust in the completed revelation found in the Bible, where all that is necessary for life and godliness has already been provided.

Foundational Questions on Scripture and Divine Communication:

1. Is Scripture sufficient?

Wouldn't you agree that "sufficient" must either mean sufficient or insufficient? There can be no middle ground.

If we accept that Scripture is sufficient, as 1 Timothy 3:16 argues, then the very notion of needing additional personal communication from God becomes both unnecessary and problematic. To claim that God still speaks directly to individuals today implies that Scripture is somehow incomplete or inadequate, a view that contradicts Paul's teaching.

Moreover, the very nature of Scripture as *God-breathed* suggests that it carries a unique authority that cannot be matched by personal revelations, impressions, or mystical experiences. Any claim of new divine communication would inherently fall short of the authority and sufficiency of Scripture, as it would either add to or contradict what has already been revealed.

According to 2 Timothy 3:17, the purpose of this divine inspiration is *"that the man of God may be perfect, thoroughly furnished unto all good works."* This verse underscores that Scripture equips believers fully—thoroughly—for every good work. There is no mention of an ongoing need for extra-biblical revelation.

2. What were the requirements for scripture?

Not everything claimed to be spoken by God was accepted as divinely inspired. The canon of Scripture was carefully established based on strict criteria: apostolic authorship or close association with the apostles, doctrinal consistency, and widespread acceptance by the early church.

Many works that claimed divine inspiration were excluded because they failed to meet these criteria. For example, the *Gospel of Thomas* and *The Shepherd of Hermas* were rejected because they contained teachings inconsistent with the core doctrines of the faith. Similarly, the *Epistle of Barnabas* and *1 Clement*, though valued by some early Christians, were not recognized as authoritative Scripture.

This process of discernment highlights the closed nature of divine revelation. After the apostolic age, no further claims of divine communication were considered to be on the level of the authoritative Word of God.

3. Is there enough general wisdom in the scripture to help a person make all of the decisions of life without receiving extra-biblical revelation or confirmation?

   If Scripture is truly sufficient, as it claims to be, then it provides all the wisdom necessary for every aspect of life. 2 Timothy 3:16-17 makes it clear that Scripture equips the believer *"thoroughly unto all good works."* This includes decisions about daily life—whether about relationships, career, or moral choices.

   While some might seek specific guidance on things like choosing a spouse or buying a house, Scripture provides all the principles necessary to make wise and godly decisions in these areas. The Bible offers timeless wisdom about character, integrity, stewardship, and

Randy White

relationships, which, when applied, guide believers in every area of life.

There is no need for extra-biblical revelation or a direct word from God about specific decisions. The Word of God already provides the wisdom we need. The pursuit of additional revelation outside of Scripture suggests that the Bible is somehow incomplete or insufficient, which contradicts its own claim of sufficiency. Thus, we don't need a "special word" about a house, a spouse, or any other personal matter. The principles found in Scripture are more than enough to guide us in every decision of life. In fact, seeking an additional word may just be indicative of our own indecision. After all, wouldn't handwriting on the wall be comforting when we make a major decision?

4. Did any of the apostles encourage or teach about receiving divine communication?

The apostles, in their writings, did not encourage ongoing, personal divine communication beyond the teachings they had already delivered. Instead, they emphasized the completeness and sufficiency of what had been revealed to them by Christ and through the Holy Spirit. For instance, Jude 1:3 urges believers to *"earnestly contend for the faith which was once delivered unto the saints,"* implying that the faith had already been fully revealed.

While the apostles did experience and acknowledge extraordinary communications from God in their time— such as visions, prophecy, and direct revelation—these were foundational to the establishment of the church and the completion of Scripture. Nowhere in their epistles do they encourage believers to seek additional, ongoing revelation as a normal Christian practice. Instead, they pointed believers to the teachings of Scripture and the work of the Holy Spirit to guide them in understanding and applying God's Word.

Some passages, such as 1 Corinthians 14, reference prophecy within the early church. However, these instances occurred during a unique transitional period when the New Testament was not yet completed. These gifts functioned as temporary confirmations of the apostles' message until the full revelation of Scripture was given.

Paul's later letters, such as 2 Timothy 3:16-17, make it clear that the inspired Scriptures are now sufficient for all instruction, correction, and equipping for good works. This further suggests that the apostles saw the written Word as the complete revelation from God, without any need for new divine communication beyond the close of the apostolic age.

Questions Concerning Historical and Biblical Context:

1. Was There Ever a Time in Which It Was Common for God to Speak to All Believers?

   Throughout biblical history, divine communication was always exceptional, not normative. God spoke to specific individuals—prophets, judges, and apostles—at key moments to deliver His message to the people. Even during these periods, direct communication from God was reserved for a select few, not the general population of believers. For instance, the prophets in the Old Testament and the apostles in the New Testament

Randy White

served as unique channels of revelation, but ordinary believers were not commonly spoken to directly by God. The communication that did occur was primarily through these appointed individuals for the benefit of the wider community, not every individual believer.

2. When God Spoke in the Past, Were the Recipients of His Word Able to Know That It Was Definitely Divine Communication?

When God spoke in the past, His communication was clear, unmistakable, and often accompanied by supernatural signs or circumstances that left no doubt about its divine origin. For example, Moses encountered God through the burning bush, a miraculous event that removed any question about the source of the communication (Exodus 3). Similarly, Paul's encounter on the road to Damascus was marked by a blinding light and a voice from heaven, leaving him with no uncertainty that it was God speaking (Acts 9:3-6). In these and other biblical accounts, recipients knew without doubt that God was speaking to them, often because the communication was miraculous or accompanied by direct supernatural signs.

This high standard of clarity and certainty raises questions for those today who claim that God speaks to them in more subtle, subjective ways, such as through feelings, impressions, or inner voices. In contrast, biblical examples of divine communication leave no room for ambiguity.

3. Is There Any Passage in Scripture Which Indicates Personal Directives Coming From God?

While there are instances in Scripture where God gave personal directives to individuals, these directives were always for specific, extraordinary purposes tied to God's redemptive plan. For example, in Genesis 12, God called Abraham to leave his home and go to a land He would show him—a directive that had profound implications for the unfolding of God's covenant with Israel. Similarly, in Acts 9, God personally directed Ananias to seek out Paul after his conversion to heal and restore his sight.

While these examples show that God did give personal directives in the past, these instances were extraordinary, not normative. They were typically tied to pivotal moments in salvation history, not everyday decisions like choosing a spouse, career, or home. There is no evidence in Scripture that God's people were regularly receiving personal directives for daily decisions. Instead, they were expected to live by the wisdom and instruction provided through God's revealed Word.

The Nature of Divine Communication:

1. If God Speaks, and It Is Inerrant, Shouldn't It Be Accepted on the Level of Scripture?

   If we believe that God still speaks today, and that such communication is truly from God, it must be inerrant. Scripture teaches that God's Word is *"God-breathed"* (2 Timothy 3:16), meaning it carries divine authority and is without error. If God were to speak again in the same way He spoke to the prophets and apostles, that revelation would have to be considered inerrant and, logically, on the same level as Scripture.

   However, treating modern claims of divine communication as equal to Scripture creates a significant theological dilemma. If God's words are indeed perfect and authoritative, any new revelation today would need to be held to the same standard as the Bible. But this raises the problem of potential contradictions or subjective interpretations. If multiple people claim to receive personal words from God, how do we determine their validity, especially if their messages conflict? This undermines the unified and final authority of the Bible, which is already complete and sufficient for all matters of life and faith.

To argue that God speaks inerrantly at times and more casually at others is theologically problematic. God does not speak *"on a whim"* or in ways that can be questioned or dismissed. In contrast, the Pope's claims of speaking *"ex-cathedra"* (with divine authority) and at other times without such authority introduce a problematic duality. God, being perfect, does not speak with such duality. His Word, whenever given, must be inerrant and authoritative. Therefore, any claim of modern divine communication must either be fully authoritative—on par with Scripture—or not divine at all. The introduction of any new revelation would necessitate expanding the canon, something that the early church decisively closed.

2. Were Extra-Biblical Works Claimed by Their Authors to Be a Word from God? If So, Why Were They Not Included in the Canon of Scripture?

Throughout history, many writings have been claimed as divine, but they were not accepted into the biblical canon. Works like the *Gospel of Thomas*, *The Shepherd of Hermas*, and *The Epistle of Barnabas* were revered by some early Christians, and their authors or followers may have believed them to be inspired. However, the early church excluded these works because they did not meet the strict criteria for canonization: apostolic authorship or close connection to the apostles, doctrinal consistency, and broad acceptance by the Christian community.

This selective process demonstrates the early church's discernment in identifying which writings truly came from God. These rejected works, though sometimes historically insightful, did not carry the same weight or authority as Scripture. The closed canon signifies that no further writings—regardless of claims of divine inspiration—can be added to Scripture. The church recognized that God's revelation was complete, and that additional claims of divine communication could not meet the standard of inerrancy or consistency required for inclusion in the canon.

Practical and Psychological Considerations:

1. If a person follows the wisdom of Scripture, will he or she make God-honoring decisions?

    The Bible provides clear principles for making godly decisions in all areas of life. 2 Timothy 3:16-17 assures us that Scripture equips the believer *"thoroughly unto all good works,"* meaning it offers sufficient wisdom to guide every decision in a way that honors God. If a person faithfully follows the teachings of Scripture— seeking wisdom from its pages and applying its moral and ethical principles—they are equipped to make decisions that align with God's will, without needing additional communication from Him.

Randy White

The Bible is filled with practical guidance on matters such as relationships, finances, work ethic, and character. It provides wisdom on how to live a life pleasing to God, from the Proverbs' teachings on wise decision-making to Paul's instructions on living a life of integrity and love. By following these timeless principles, believers can be confident they are making decisions that honor God.

The desire for extra-biblical confirmation often arises from a sense of uncertainty or fear of making the wrong choice, but Scripture provides all the wisdom needed to navigate life's challenges. The Bible calls believers to trust God's inspired Word. As Psalm 119:105 declares, *"Thy word is a lamp unto my feet, and a light unto my path."* The Scriptures illuminate our way, giving us the tools to make wise, God-honoring decisions without the need for additional divine communication.

2. Does a Good Outcome in Decision-Making Indicate Divine Favor or Guidance?

It's common to attribute positive outcomes to divine favor or guidance, but this raises the question: do responsible decisions always reflect God's direct involvement, or are they more a product of wisdom, common sense, and personal responsibility? This applies both to believers and unbelievers alike, as people across all walks of life make decisions that result in positive outcomes without necessarily claiming divine intervention.

Wise decision-making, based on principles such as diligence, integrity, and careful planning—many of which are also taught in Scripture—naturally leads to better outcomes. Both believers and unbelievers who exercise responsibility and sound judgment are likely to see successful results in their lives. Jesus Himself noted in Matthew 5:45 that God *"maketh His sun to rise on the evil and on the good, and sendeth rain on the just and on the unjust."* In other words, good outcomes often follow natural law and common wisdom, not necessarily divine favor.

While believers might be tempted to interpret success as a direct result of God's specific guidance, it is important to recognize that God has already given general wisdom in Scripture that applies to everyone. Whether a believer or unbeliever applies these principles—such as hard work (Proverbs 14:23), careful planning (Proverbs 21:5), or honesty (Proverbs 11:3)— good outcomes can result.

Thus, a favorable outcome is not always evidence of direct divine communication or favor. Instead, it can often be attributed to practical wisdom and sound decision-making, which God has embedded in His natural laws and moral principles. This distinction prevents us from assuming that good results always signify divine approval or special guidance, especially when the Bible provides sufficient wisdom for making responsible choices.

3. Does the Tendency to "Receive" Divine Communication Depend on One's Belief in It, and Could This Indicate Psychological Influence?

It is often observed that those who believe in ongoing divine communication report experiencing it, while those who do not believe in it rarely claim such experiences. This pattern can be seen across various religions and denominations, with claims of divine communication

Randy White

appearing to align with a group's theological or cultural expectations. This raises the question: *could these experiences be influenced by the power of the psyche rather than an actual divine source?*

Psychology suggests that people are deeply affected by their beliefs and expectations. When a person is immersed in an environment that affirms divine communication, they may be more inclined to interpret certain thoughts, feelings, or impressions as coming from God. This can create a feedback loop, where belief reinforces experience, and experience strengthens belief, regardless of whether the communication is objectively divine.

Additionally, cultural and religious contexts play a significant role in shaping how individuals perceive and interpret spiritual experiences. For instance, those within charismatic or Pentecostal circles often report more frequent divine communication, whereas those from cessationist backgrounds, who do not expect such communication, rarely claim to receive it. This pattern transcends Christian denominations and is evident in various religions, where divine communication or mystical experiences are reported based on cultural and religious expectations.

While this does not entirely disprove the possibility of divine communication, it does raise valid questions about the influence of psychological factors. The human mind is powerful in its ability to create experiences that align with deeply held beliefs. This calls for caution in attributing such experiences solely to divine origin, as they may be heavily shaped by personal expectation and cultural conditioning.

4. Have You Ever Been Scared of or Convinced of Something That Absolutely Was Not There?

Human perception is notoriously susceptible to errors, leading people to believe in things that are not real. Many of us have experienced fear or conviction about something that later proved to be entirely unfounded. Whether it's hearing a noise in the dark and imagining danger, or being convinced of a misunderstanding, these moments illustrate how our minds can deceive us, particularly when emotions and expectations are involved.

This susceptibility to mistaken perceptions is highly relevant when evaluating claims of divine communication. Just as fear can make us believe in threats that aren't there, strong religious or emotional expectations can lead people to interpret internal impressions, feelings, or coincidences as direct communication from God. The mind is powerful in shaping perceptions based on belief, and this can cause individuals to be sincerely convinced they have received a divine message, even when there is no objective basis for it.

This doesn't necessarily imply dishonesty or deliberate fabrication, but rather highlights the human tendency to interpret subjective experiences in line with deeply held beliefs. Whether through fear, expectation, or cultural influence, our perceptions can often lead us to believe in things that are simply not there. In the case of divine communication, this opens the possibility that some experiences may be psychological rather than supernatural.

Randy White

Chapter 2:

How Churches Promote "Hearing from God"

The promotion of the concept of "hearing from God" is ubiquitous. Virtually all forms of Christianity have a "How to hear from God" doctrine and accept the view that God still communicates, whether generally or specifically, with Christians today. While for some denominational families this is almost a bedrock belief, only a handful of denominational families forbid the practice.

Extreme Examples

Let's begin with examples that are rejected by most mainstream Christianity but illustrate where this concept can lead. Just because mainstream Christianity doesn't go as far as these extremes doesn't mean the problem doesn't exist, as we shall soon see.

The Church of Jesus Christ of Latter-Day Saints

One of the most prominent and extreme examples of claims to "hearing from God" is found in the history of The Church of Jesus Christ of Latter-day Saints (LDS Church), founded by Joseph Smith in the early 19th century.

The First Vision

In the spring of 1820, at the age of 14, Joseph Smith reported experiencing what is now known as the First Vision. Seeking spiritual guidance amid the religious revivalism of the time, Smith prayed in a wooded area near his home in Palmyra, New York. According to his account, he was visited by God the Father and Jesus Christ, who instructed him that all existing churches had strayed from true Christianity. This vision is considered the foundational event of the LDS Church, establishing Smith's role as a prophet chosen to restore the original church.

The Book of Mormon

Building on his initial vision, Joseph Smith claimed that in 1823 an angel named Moroni appeared to him, revealing the location of buried golden plates inscribed with an ancient record. Over the next several years, Smith reported receiving divine instructions to retrieve and translate these plates. Using seer stones placed in a hat to block out light, Smith translated the text into what became the **Book of Mormon**, published in 1830. This book is presented by the LDS Church as another testament of Jesus Christ, complementing the Bible.

Additional Visions and Revelations

Beyond the First Vision and the Book of Mormon, Joseph Smith reported numerous other visions and revelations that guided the formation and doctrinal development of the LDS Church:

- **The Restoration of Priesthood Authority:** Smith asserted that he and his associates were visited by John the Baptist and later by apostles Peter, James, and John, who conferred upon them the priesthood authority necessary to lead the church.

- **Temple Revelations:** Smith received detailed instructions for building temples, which are considered sacred spaces for essential ordinances. These revelations also included ceremonies such as baptism for the dead and eternal marriage.

- ◆ **The Doctrine and Covenants:** This collection of revelations covers various aspects of church governance, doctrine, and practice, further illustrating ongoing divine communication.

- ◆ **Visions of Future Events:** Smith provided prophetic insights into future events, including the establishment of Zion, the Second Coming of Christ, and the gathering of Israel.

Impact and Controversy

Joseph Smith's claims to divine communication and the extraordinary experiences he reported have made the LDS Church both a significant religious movement and a subject of controversy. Mainstream Christianity generally rejects these claims, viewing them as outside orthodox beliefs. Nonetheless, within the LDS community, these visions are seen as evidence of continuing revelation and God's active involvement in guiding His followers.

By examining Joseph Smith's experiences, we observe how the concept of "hearing from God" can lead to the formation of new religious traditions and doctrines. These extreme examples highlight the profound influence such claims can have, both within their own communities and in the broader religious landscape.

The Quakers

Another significant example of a Christian group that emphasizes direct communication with God is the Religious Society of Friends, commonly known as the Quakers. Originating in 17th-century England, Quakerism places a strong emphasis on personal, inner experiences of the divine, often eschewing formal creeds and liturgies in favor of silent worship and spontaneous expressions of faith.

Quaker Worship and Seeking the Word from God

Quaker meetings for worship are typically held in silence, allowing individuals to seek and listen for the "Inner Light"—a divine presence believed to reside within each person. Participants may speak if they feel moved by the Spirit, sharing messages or insights they believe are inspired by God. This form of worship aims to facilitate a direct and personal connection with the divine, without the need for intermediaries such as clergy or sacraments.

While mainstream Quakerism emphasizes personal and communal discernment over extraordinary claims, there have been instances where individual Quakers have reported profound or unusual experiences of divine communication. Some of these can be considered extreme within the broader Quaker tradition.

Impact and Controversy

The Quakers' emphasis on personal revelation and the Inner Light fosters a deeply individualistic approach to faith, which can lead to a wide variety of spiritual experiences. While most Quaker practices remain within the bounds of silent worship and communal discernment, the instances of prophetic voices and charismatic expressions illustrate how the desire to hear from God can push the boundaries of traditional belief and practice.

Quakerism demonstrates that the concept of "hearing from God" is not confined to fringe movements but can manifest in diverse ways even within established religious traditions.

Randy White

Oral Roberts

Another notable example of an individual claiming to "hear from God" comes from Oral Roberts, a prominent American televangelist and faith healer who played a significant role in the rise of the charismatic movement in the mid-20th century. Founded in the 1940s, Oral Roberts Ministries emphasized divine healing, prosperity and direct communication with God, attracting millions of followers through television broadcasts and large-scale revival meetings.

Hearing from God: The Million-Dollar Miracle

One of the most extreme and widely publicized instances of Oral Roberts claiming to hear directly from God involves his famous **"Million-Dollar Miracle."** In the early 1950s, facing financial difficulties in expanding his ministry, Roberts reported receiving a divine instruction to raise one million dollars in a single year. Believing this was a direct command from God, he launched an extensive fundraising campaign that included nationwide tent meetings, radio broadcasts, and personal appeals to his followers.

Roberts's appeal resonated deeply with his audience, who believed that their financial contributions would not only support the ministry but also be part of a miraculous divine provision. Miraculously, the goal was achieved within the stipulated timeframe, which Roberts attributed to God's intervention. This event significantly boosted Roberts's credibility and expanded the reach of his ministry, setting a precedent for faith-based fundraising efforts within the charismatic movement.

The 1987 $8 Million Fundraising Appeal

In addition to the Million-Dollar Miracle, Oral Roberts made another significant fundraising appeal in 1987, which he attributed to direct divine instruction. Facing the ongoing expansion needs of his ministry, Roberts proclaimed that God had commanded him to raise $8 million within a single year to build a state-of-the-art healing center and expand his televangelism efforts. Emphasizing faith and divine provision, Roberts launched an intensive campaign that included televised sermons, personal testimonies of healing, and extensive outreach through his ministry's media channels.

The Ultimatum: Divine Consequence

During this 1987 appeal, Roberts took his plea to an extreme by asserting that God had warned him that He would call him home—a euphemism for death—if the congregation failed to meet the $8 million goal. This stark ultimatum was intended to instill a sense of urgency and compel his followers to contribute generously. By framing the fundraising target as a matter of divine consequence, Roberts leveraged both fear and faith to motivate his audience, suggesting that their financial support was directly tied to his personal well-being and the future of the ministry.

Impact and Reactions

Roberts's ultimatum had a profound impact on his followers. Many believers were deeply moved by what they perceived as a genuine divine warning, leading to a surge in donations that ultimately enabled the ministry to achieve its financial target. The success of this appeal reinforced Roberts's reputation as a prophet-like figure who could

22

directly communicate God's will, thereby strengthening the loyalty and commitment of his congregation.

However, this approach also attracted significant criticism and skepticism. Detractors argued that using the threat of personal demise to secure financial contributions was manipulative and unethical, blurring the lines between genuine spiritual leadership and coercive fundraising tactics. Critics within and outside the evangelical community questioned the theological appropriateness of linking financial support so directly with personal and organizational salvation, raising concerns about the potential for exploitation of believers' faith.

Impact and Legacy

Despite the controversies, Oral Roberts's influence on American Christianity and the broader charismatic movement is undeniable. His innovative use of media transformed evangelical outreach, setting the stage for future televangelists. The Million-Dollar Miracle exemplifies how claims of divine communication can galvanize large-scale movements and inspire significant financial contributions from followers.

Oral Roberts's legacy continues through the Oral Roberts University, founded in 1963, which remains a prominent institution for evangelical education. His life and ministry illustrate both the impact and the potential pitfalls of promoting the concept of "hearing from God" within a religious framework.

The Lack of a Boundary

The common response to extreme examples of "hearing from God"—that is, simply stating "we don't believe that"—

is insufficient to address the underlying issue. Without a clear theological boundary defining how, when, or if God speaks today, the door remains open for progressively more extreme interpretations to arise. A more robust theological framework is necessary to guard against misuse or manipulation of this concept, offering a solid foundation for discerning genuine spiritual experiences from those that may lead to doctrinal or ethical concerns. Without such boundaries, the potential for confusion and abuse grows unchecked.

Denominational Examples

Catholic Churches: Mysticism and Contemplative Practices

Catholicism has a long and rich tradition of mysticism and contemplative practices, which have been integral to its spiritual and theological development for centuries. From the early Desert Fathers and Mothers to renowned mystics like St. Teresa of Ávila, St. John of the Cross, and Meister Eckhart, the Catholic Church has consistently promoted the pursuit of direct and profound experiences of the divine. These mystics emphasized inner prayer, meditation, and the contemplation of God's presence, fostering a personal and transformative relationship with the sacred.

Throughout the Middle Ages and the Renaissance, Catholic mysticism flourished within monastic communities, where contemplative practices were seen as a path to spiritual enlightenment and union with God. The establishment of orders such as the Franciscans and the Dominicans provided structured environments for individuals to engage deeply in prayer and mystical experiences. The writings and teachings of these mystics have been celebrated and continue to influence Catholic spirituality, and in some cases have entered mainstream Protestant and evangelical acceptance.

In modern times, the Catholic Church has maintained its commitment to contemplative practices through various movements and initiatives. The rise of lay spirituality in the 20th and 21st centuries has made mysticism more accessible to the broader Catholic population, encouraging individuals to seek personal encounters with God through silent retreats, meditation, and prayer groups. Additionally, the Church has embraced contemporary expressions of mysticism, integrating insights from modern psychology and interfaith dialogue to enrich its contemplative traditions.

Pope John Paul II and Pope Francis have both underscored the value of contemplative prayer and mystical experiences in their teachings, advocating for a balanced approach that harmonizes intellectual understanding with experiential faith. The promotion of retreats, spiritual direction, and educational programs within Catholic institutions further supports the ongoing practice of seeking and hearing from God in a personal and profound manner.

Evangelical Churches: The "Still Small Voice" and Personal Impressions

In evangelical Christianity, the concept of hearing from God is often articulated through the metaphor of the "still small voice." This idea is rooted in the biblical narrative of Elijah in 1 Kings 19:12, where God communicates to him not through dramatic manifestations like fire or earthquakes, but through a gentle whisper. Evangelicals interpret this as indicative of how God typically speaks to believers today—quietly and personally, rather than through loud or miraculous signs.

The Southern Baptist Convention: A Case Study In Hearing from God

Within the Southern Baptist Convention (SBC), the "Experiencing God" movement, spearheaded by Henry Blackaby, stands out as a clear example of how the largest evangelical denomination promotes the concept of hearing from God. Originating in the late 20th century, Blackaby's teachings have deeply influenced Southern Baptists, fostering a culture where believers are actively encouraged to seek and recognize God's voice through multiple avenues.

Henry Blackaby's *"Experiencing God"*

Henry Blackaby, along with co-author Dr. Karl Matthias, introduced the *"Experiencing God"* series in the early 1980s. The core premise of this movement is that God desires a personal and dynamic relationship with each believer, characterized by active communication and collaboration. Blackaby emphasized that hearing from God is not limited to Scripture, nor to dramatic supernatural events, but encompasses everyday experiences and interactions.

The "Experiencing God" movement quickly gained traction within the SBC, resonating with pastors, church leaders, and lay members alike. Its structured approach to spiritual growth—comprising books, workshops, and seminars—provided practical tools for individuals and congregations to deepen their relationship with God. The movement's emphasis on intentional prayer, scripture study, and discerning God's will contributed to its widespread adoption and enduring influence within Southern Baptist churches.

Blackaby's framework outlined several key avenues through which believers can hear from God, each reinforcing the idea that divine guidance is accessible in various forms:

- **Through the Bible:** Central to the "Experiencing God" philosophy is the belief that scripture is God's primary means of communication. Blackaby encouraged regular and deliberate Bible study, teaching that God's word provides clear guidance, wisdom, and direction for daily living.

- **Through Prayer and Meditation:** Personal prayer and contemplative practices were emphasized as essential for tuning into God's voice. Blackaby advocated for consistent and heartfelt communication with God, fostering an environment where believers can listen and respond to His guidance.

- **Through Sermons and Teaching:** Pastors and church leaders play a crucial role in conveying God's messages during sermons and teachings. The movement encouraged leaders to preach with the intent of not only delivering biblical truths but also helping congregants recognize and apply God's voice in their lives.

- **Through Circumstances and Life Events:** Blackaby taught that God often uses life's circumstances—

both joyous and challenging—as instruments of His communication. Believers are encouraged to view their experiences as opportunities to discern God's will and purpose.

- ◆ **Through Others:** Community and fellowship are vital components of hearing from God. Blackaby emphasized the importance of seeking counsel and insight from fellow believers, mentors, and spiritual advisors who can provide confirmation and clarity regarding God's direction.

The International Mission Board's Dream Ministry

Building upon the foundational principles of the "Experiencing God" movement, the Southern Baptist Convention's International Mission Board (IMB) has often emphasized divine communication through dreams. One of the most notable aspects of the IMB's approach is its promotion of dreams to draw individuals to Christ in predominantly Muslim regions.

The IMB regularly shares testimonies from individuals in Islamic-majority countries who report having dreams in which Jesus Christ personally calls them to salvation. These accounts often describe vivid and emotionally charged experiences where the dreamer feels a direct and urgent invitation from Jesus to embrace Christianity. Such testimonies are presented as evidence of God's active efforts to communicate and guide individuals beyond traditional missionary methods.

Randy White

Dispensational Churches: Interpreting "Signs Of The Times."

Dispensationalism is a theological framework within evangelical Christianity that emphasizes a literal interpretation of biblical prophecy, particularly concerning the end times. Dispensationalism divides history into distinct periods or "dispensations," each characterized by specific divine interactions and expectations. A hallmark of a more populist dispensational thought is the belief that current events in the news and the natural world are direct indicators of prophetic fulfillment, signaling the imminent return of Jesus Christ and the establishment of God's kingdom.

While there are dispensationalists, like myself, who reject this view, the more populist form of dispensationalism, often seen on television, promotes the belief that contemporary events fulfill biblical prophecies, signaling the approaching end times. This interpretive approach leads adherents to scrutinize global developments, natural phenomena, and geopolitical shifts through a prophetic lens. Furthermore, it encourages followers of this form of dispensationalism to scour newspapers and scan the skies for the next big sign.

Several prominent examples illustrate how dispensational churches apply this framework:

One of the most notable instances of dispensational interpretation is John Hagee's "Four Blood Moons" prophecy. Hagee, a prominent evangelical pastor and founder of Christians United for Israel (CUFI), asserted that a series of four consecutive lunar eclipses, each occurring during a Jewish Passover, signified pivotal prophetic milestones. According to Hagee the alignment of these blood moons with Passover festivals was interpreted as a divine sign indicating the nearing fulfillment of end-time prophecies. The Four Blood Moons prophecy gained widespread attention within evangelical circles, reinforcing the desire to look to current events as a word from God.

Books like *"The Late Great Planet Earth"* by Hal Lindsey interpreted signs of the end times in every financial downturn, moral lapse, political instability, and technological advance. Published in 1970, this book sparked a period of heightened vigilance for apocalyptic signs. While this quest for omens and harbingers differs from some forms of "hearing from God," it nonetheless affirms the belief that God actively communicates with humanity today.

And, just like all the other methods of hearing the "voices" from heaven, dispensationalist interpretations have always been speculative and exaggerated predictions that have lead to disappointment and disillusionment when prophecies do not manifest as expected.

Fundamental Churches: "Prompting of the Spirit" and Subjective Experiences

Within the spectrum of Christian denominations, Fundamental churches occupy a distinct position regarding the concept of hearing from God. Unlike most denominational or charismatic movements that may emphasize prophetic revelations or the "still small voice," Fundamental churches typically refrain from endorsing formal prophecies or overt divine communications.

Instead, they focus on the "prompting of the Spirit" and highly value subjective experiences as means through which believers perceive God's guidance and presence.

Fundamental churches uphold the Bible as the sole infallible word of God, adhering to biblical inerrancy and doctrinal purity. In this context, hearing from God is understood primarily through the internal promptings of the Holy Spirit, rather than external manifestations or prophetic utterances. While more subtle, this approach still constitutes a form of extra-biblical revelation. These churches recognize and celebrate subjective experiences interpreted as manifestations of God's presence and guidance. Believers often describe these in deeply personal terms, such as "I felt it deep in my soul" or "I sensed God's direction." Furthermore, strong emotional reactions during sermons, worship services, or personal devotion times are often seen as the Holy Spirit moving within them, reinforcing their faith and commitment. Without clear boundaries, there is a potential for believers to misinterpret personal feelings or emotions as divine guidance, leading to decisions that may not align with biblical principles.

Virtually Everywhere

The concept of "hearing from God" is nearly universal across Christian denominations, each presenting its own way in which divine communication goes beyond Scripture itself. While the Bible is revered as the ultimate authority in almost all of Christianity, most traditions embrace the idea that God continues to guide, inspire, and communicate with believers through other means. Whether it's through mystical experiences in Catholicism, the "still small voice" in evangelical churches, dreams in missions work, or even the promptings of the Spirit in Fundamental churches, the belief that God speaks to His followers remains central.

These practices often involve some form of personal, internal experience—whether emotional, spiritual, or even circumstantial. Individuals across denominations are taught to discern God's voice through prayer, meditation, sermons, community interactions, or subjective impressions. While the manner of discerning and validating such communications differs, most Christians are open to the idea that God is not silent but actively engaging with His people in their everyday lives.

This widespread acceptance of hearing from God— whether through dreams, impressions, inner promptings, or "signs of the times"—illustrates how deeply embedded this concept is in Christian spirituality. Even though specific methods may vary, the underlying belief that God continues to interact with His people in ways beyond Scripture remains a common thread in Christian practice, crossing denominational lines. The near-universal endorsement of this belief opens the door to extremes, as we have seen, but also leaves mainstream Christian communities with little to no theological boundary in determining how—or if—God speaks today.

Those Who Do Not Hear From God

There are Christian groups that emphasize the principle of sola scriptura (Scripture alone) so strongly that they reject any claim of direct communication from God outside of the Bible. These groups assert that the canon of Scripture is closed and that God speaks solely through His written

Word. While they may believe in the work of the Holy Spirit in illuminating the meaning of Scripture for believers, they reject the idea of receiving new prophecies, revelations, or subjective "words from God" beyond what is explicitly stated in the Bible. Some examples include:

1. Reformed and Confessional Churches

   While I reject Reformed theology, it is true that many Reformed churches, particularly those holding tightly to historical confessions like the Westminster Confession of Faith, reject extra-biblical revelations. These groups emphasize that God has fully and finally spoken through Scripture, and any claim of direct divine communication beyond the Bible is considered unnecessary or even dangerous. They maintain that the Bible alone is sufficient for all matters of faith and practice.

   For example, John Calvin, one of the key figures in the Reformation, emphasized the finality of God's revelation in Scripture. The Westminster Confession also states, "The whole counsel of God concerning all things necessary for his own glory, man's salvation, faith, and life, is either expressly set down in Scripture, or by good and necessary consequence may be deduced from Scripture unto which nothing at any time is to be added, whether by new revelations of the Spirit, or traditions of men." However, the Confession does go on to say, "Nevertheless, we acknowledge the inward illumination of the Spirit of God to be necessary for the saving understanding of such things as are revealed in the Word." While this "inward illumination" is far from the hearing from God promoted by non reformed churches, it does insist that a person cannot hear from God through God's Word without special illumination.

2. Cessationist Baptists and Bible Churches

   Certain Baptist and independent Bible churches, especially those adhering to cessationism, hold that the miraculous gifts of the Spirit—such as prophecy, tongues, and direct revelation—ceased after the apostolic era. These groups teach that Scripture is sufficient and that the kind of direct divine communication often seen in charismatic or evangelical circles is no longer in operation. The degree of cessationism varies, as does the robustness of their cessationist arguments.

   Certain Fundamentalist groups also take a hard stance against any form of divine revelation outside of Scripture. They emphasize the inerrancy, infallibility, and sufficiency of the Bible and warn against the dangers of personal revelations, prophecies, or subjective spiritual experiences. These groups may acknowledge the role of the Holy Spirit in helping believers understand and apply the Bible, but they strictly limit the concept of "hearing from God" to Scripture alone.

3. Some Branches of Lutheranism

   Some **Lutheran** groups, particularly those aligned with the **Confessional Lutheran** tradition, hold that Scripture alone is the means by which God speaks. While they recognize the role of the Holy Spirit in leading Christians into all truth, they reject modern revelations or "words from God" as extraneous to the already complete and sufficient revelation given in Scripture.

4. Exclusive Brethren

   The Exclusive Brethren are another example of a group that adheres strictly to the principle that God's word is contained entirely within the Bible. They typically reject any concept of extra-biblical revelation, focusing on the inerrancy and sufficiency of Scripture for all matters of life and godliness.

5. Mid-Acts and Acts 28 Dispensationalism

Mid-Acts dispensationalists believe that the Church, the Body of Christ, began with the ministry of the Apostle Paul, specifically in Acts 9 (the conversion of Paul) or Acts 13 (Paul's first missionary journey). This view holds that prior to Paul's ministry, the gospel preached was the Gospel of the Kingdom, aimed at Israel. Paul introduced the Gospel of Grace, which is the message for the Church in this present dispensation.

Mid-Acts dispensationalists typically hold to cessationist views, rejecting the continuation of the miraculous gifts like tongues, prophecy, and healing after the apostolic age. They emphasize that the full revelation of God is found in the Pauline epistles and the broader New Testament, and they do not advocate for any direct communication from God beyond Scripture.

Acts 28 dispensationalists take an even more specific view, believing that the Church, the Body of Christ, began after the close of the book of Acts, at Acts 28. They argue that Paul's earlier ministry was still tied to the Kingdom program for Israel, and that the full revelation of the mystery concerning the Church was not made known until his later epistles, written after Acts 28.

Like Mid-Acts dispensationalists, Acts 28 adherents are strongly cessationist and hold that God no longer speaks through modern-day revelations, dreams, or prophecies. For them, Paul's later epistles (like Ephesians, Philippians, and Colossians) contain the final and complete revelation for the Church, and they reject any notion of receiving additional guidance or revelation beyond the completed canon of Scripture.

Conclusion

Though the concept of hearing from God is widespread in Christianity, these groups emphasize a closed canon of Scripture and hold that God communicates exclusively through the Bible. They see claims of modern revelations, promptings, or extra-biblical words from God as either mistaken, unnecessary, or even harmful, as they believe it can lead believers away from the final authority of the written Word.

CHAPTER 3:

The Psychology of Hearing Voices

The experience of hearing "voices" is more common than many people realize. Studies suggest that a significant portion of the population will, at some point in their lives, hear voices that others do not hear. These auditory experiences can range from hearing one's name called when no one is around to more complex dialogues with unseen speakers. While sometimes associated with mental health conditions, hearing voices can also occur in the absence of any psychiatric disorder. Stress, grief, fatigue, and intense emotional states can all contribute to such experiences.

Understanding that hearing voices is a widespread phenomenon helps demystify it. It is a part of the human experience that reflects the incredible complexity of our minds. Our brains are capable of creating vivid sensory experiences without external stimuli, blurring the lines between perception and reality. Recognizing this normalcy is the first step toward a compassionate and informed approach to the topic.

For people of faith, hearing voices often takes on a spiritual significance. Many attribute these experiences to divine guidance, believing that God is speaking directly to them. This interpretation can offer comfort, direction, and a sense of purpose. However, it also raises important questions about how we discern the source of these voices and align them with our understanding of God's communication through Scripture.

Emphasizing the importance of this topic within the context of faith, we must carefully examine the phenomenon from both psychological and theological perspectives. By doing so, we can appreciate the intricacies of the human mind while upholding the belief that God's primary mode of communication is through His Word. This balanced understanding helps prevent confusion and potential mental health challenges that may arise from misinterpreting these experiences.

The primary aim of this chapter is to delve into the psychological underpinnings of hearing voices, particularly those that individuals interpret as divine guidance. By examining the mental processes and emotional states that contribute to auditory experiences, we can gain a clearer understanding of why some believers might perceive these voices as messages from God. This exploration is crucial for several reasons.

Firstly, by uncovering the psychological explanations behind hearing voices, we can demystify the phenomenon. Understanding that these voices can stem from natural mental functions—such as the brain's ability to process stress, grief, or intense desire and emotions—provides a well-grounded perspective on these experiences. This knowledge empowers individuals to approach their experiences with greater self-awareness and less mysticism, fear, or confusion.

Secondly, this chapter seeks to establish a clear distinction between normal psychological occurrences and what might be considered genuine divine communication. While personal spiritual experiences are an integral part of faith, it is essential to discern whether these experiences

Randy White

align with biblical teachings or stem from internal psychological states. By providing criteria and insights into this differentiation process, the chapter equips readers with the tools to evaluate their own experiences critically.

Moreover, addressing the psychological aspects of hearing voices aligns with the book's broader objective of affirming that God's communication is exclusively through Scripture. By highlighting how inner desires and fears can manifest as auditory experiences, the chapter reinforces the notion that true divine messages are consistent with biblical revelation rather than subjective or isolated experiences.

Ultimately, the purpose of this chapter is to bridge the gap between faith and psychology, offering a balanced perspective that honors both the complexity of the human mind and the sufficiency of God's Word. By doing so, it aims to foster a healthier, more informed approach to understanding and interpreting experiences of hearing voices within a faith context.

My thesis in this chapter is that hearing voices and attributing them to divine guidance reflects inner desires and fears and can serve as a coping mechanism. However, when these experiences are not understood as psychological phenomena, they can lead to emerging mental health issues. This chapter argues that recognizing the psychological roots of auditory experiences is essential for maintaining both spiritual integrity and mental well-being. By distinguishing between natural mental processes and genuine divine communication, believers can navigate their spiritual journeys with clarity and support, preventing the potential negative consequences that arise from misinterpreting these voices.

Understanding Auditory Hallucinations

Definition and Nature

Auditory hallucinations are experiences where individuals hear sounds, most commonly voices, that have no external source. From a psychological standpoint, these voices can vary widely in their nature and impact. They may range from simple sounds, like hearing one's name called, to complex dialogues involving multiple speakers. These auditory experiences are not confined to any particular demographic and can occur across different age groups, cultures, and backgrounds.

Psychologically, auditory hallucinations are understood as perceptions that arise without corresponding external stimuli. They result from the brain's intricate processes of interpreting and generating sensory information. The phenomenon can be dissected into two primary categories: pathological and non-pathological auditory hallucinations.

Pathological Auditory Hallucinations are typically associated with mental health disorders. Conditions such as schizophrenia, bipolar disorder, and severe depression often feature auditory hallucinations as a symptom. In these cases, the voices can be distressing, commanding, or abusive, significantly impacting the individual's ability to function daily. Pathological hallucinations are usually persistent and may require clinical intervention, including therapy and medication, to manage their effects.

On the other hand, **Non-Pathological Auditory Hallucinations** occur in the absence of any diagnosed

40

psychiatric condition. These experiences are relatively common, almost all of us have them, and can be triggered by various factors such as extreme stress, grief, sleep deprivation, or intense emotional states. For example, individuals who are grieving may hear the voice of a lost loved one, providing comfort during a difficult time. Similarly, those under significant stress might hear voices that offer reassurance or direction, functioning as a coping mechanism to navigate challenging circumstances.

In addition to the typical auditory experiences, hallucinations can also manifest in more subtle ways. Some individuals describe their experience **"as if it were audible,"** where they do not hear a literal external voice but perceive it with such vividness that it feels as though it was spoken aloud. Others may express the sensation as **"I know I was prompted,"** where there is no clear sound but rather a strong internal sense of guidance or direction, often interpreted as communication from God. These experiences, though less direct than hearing an actual voice, are still rooted in the brain's capacity to generate perceived communication in the absence of external stimuli.

The distinction between pathological and non-pathological auditory hallucinations, along with these subtler forms, lies primarily in their context and impact. While pathological hallucinations are indicative of underlying mental health issues and often require professional treatment, non-pathological and "as if audible" experiences are generally transient and linked to specific psychological states or environmental factors. Understanding this differentiation is crucial, especially within a faith context, as it allows individuals and communities to approach these experiences with compassion and appropriate responses, ensuring that those who need help receive it without stigma.

By comprehensively defining and distinguishing the nature of auditory hallucinations, we lay the groundwork for further exploration into how these experiences intersect with faith and the potential psychological implications they carry. This understanding is essential for discerning whether such voices align with communication from God or stem from natural psychological processes.

Prevalence and Normalcy of Auditory Hallucinations

Auditory hallucinations, while often associated with mental health disorders, are more common in the general population than many realize. According to a study involving 10,448 participants, a significant portion of individuals report having experienced auditory hallucinations at some point in their lives.

- **44.1%** of respondents indicated that they have *never* experienced auditory hallucinations. Thus, over almost 55% of the population has these experiences.

- **26.3%** of participants reported that they had experienced auditory hallucinations in the past, but not within the last month.

- **14.7%** of individuals stated that they had experienced auditory hallucinations within the past month, but not in the last week. This subset of the population experiences such phenomena on a somewhat regular, but not constant, basis.

◆ Finally, **14.9%** of respondents experienced auditory hallucinations within the past week, indicating that for a notable portion of people, these experiences are a more immediate and ongoing part of life.[1]

These statistics highlight the normalcy of auditory hallucinations in various forms. While some experience them rarely, others encounter them more frequently, suggesting that auditory hallucinations are a widespread phenomenon that occurs under a range of conditions and does not always indicate underlying pathology. This understanding of the prevalence of such experiences helps to demystify them, framing auditory hallucinations as part of the broader spectrum of normal human psychological experiences.

Trigger Points

Several significant triggers can lead to auditory hallucinations. Often, when individuals believe God has spoken to them, they are experiencing one or more of these trigger points in their lives.

1. Stress:

   One of the most prevalent triggers of auditory hallucinations is stress. Under high-pressure situations, the mind may attempt to cope with overwhelming emotions by manifesting sounds or voices. These hallucinations often serve as a psychological release, providing a sense of direction or reassurance when a person feels lost or unsure. For example, during

---

1 Linszen, Maya M. J., *et al.* "Occurrence and Phenomenology of Hallucinations in the General Population: A Large Online Survey." npj Schizophrenia, vol. 8, no. 1, 2022, p. 26. Nature, *https://www.nature.com/articles/s41537-022-00229-9*. Accessed 20 Sept. 2024.

a period of intense stress—whether due to work, personal relationships, or health concerns—individuals might hear voices that seem to offer guidance or comfort. While the brain creates these experiences, they are often interpreted as external messages, sometimes even attributed to divine intervention.

2. Fatigue:

Prolonged fatigue or sleep deprivation can also lead to auditory hallucinations. When the brain is deprived of rest, its ability to process sensory information accurately begins to deteriorate. This can lead to the misinterpretation of normal internal sounds (like thoughts or inner dialogue) as external auditory stimuli. In some cases, individuals report hearing their name called or simple auditory cues, such as the ringing of a phone or knocking, when no such sounds are present. These hallucinations are often brief and dissipate once the person has rested, but they underscore how exhaustion can blur the lines between reality and illusion.

3. Grief:

Grief, especially after the loss of a loved one, is another powerful trigger for auditory hallucinations. Many individuals who are grieving report hearing the voice of the deceased, particularly in the early stages of their mourning. This phenomenon is the mind's way of processing loss and keeping the memory of the loved one alive during a painful emotional transition. The hallucinations can offer temporary comfort, giving the grieving person a sense of continued connection with their loved one. While this type of auditory experience is often harmless and transient, it is deeply tied to the emotional weight of loss.

44

4. Intense Desire:

Intense desires or fixations can also trigger auditory hallucinations or internal prompts that feel as though they are externally sourced. When someone strongly desires something, such as an expensive product, a particular outcome, or the fulfillment of a deep personal longing, the mind may generate internal voices or impressions that align with these desires. These experiences often seem to provide external encouragement or validation, pushing the individual toward acting on their desire.

For instance, a person considering a costly purchase might "hear" a voice or feel a strong sense of being prompted to move forward, reinforcing their emotional connection to the object of their desire. In such cases, the auditory experience is not a sign of divine guidance but rather an internal reflection of the individual's emotional and psychological investment in the desired outcome.

How the Brain Generates Voices Through Internal Thought Processes

Our minds are constantly at work, processing thoughts, emotions, and sensory information. Sometimes, this can result in the perception of voices or sounds that aren't actually coming from outside our bodies. Here's how that happens:

1. Inner Speech and Mistaken Perception:

We all engage in what's called "inner speech"—that little voice inside our heads when we think or plan something. The parts of our brain that handle this inner dialogue are the same ones that process real, external sounds. Sometimes, however, the brain gets confused and treats these internal thoughts as if they were actual sounds coming from the outside. This is why someone might feel like they've "heard" something, when it's really just their own thoughts being misinterpreted as audible.

2. **The Auditory Part of the Brain Acting on Its Own:**

   Our brains can generate sounds or voices even without external noise. The part of the brain responsible for hearing, called the auditory cortex, can become active on its own due to random brain activity. This can create the sensation of hearing voices or sounds that aren't actually present. Sometimes, thoughts or other senses can accidentally "wake up" this part of the brain, causing these auditory experiences. (**Note:** this is different from things like Tinnitus, which are false sound signals sent to the brain from the ear itself).

3. **Chemical Imbalances in the Brain:**

   Our brain's chemistry, especially the levels of a chemical called dopamine, plays a role in how we interpret thoughts and sensations. When there's too much dopamine activity in certain areas of the brain, it can make normal, internal thoughts feel much more important or "real" than they actually are. As a result, a person might believe their own thoughts are external voices, making it seem like they are hearing something from outside.

   Common triggers for dopamine imbalances include **stress**, which can increase dopamine production in response to pressure; **substance use**, such as stimulants or drugs like amphetamines and cocaine, which directly affect dopamine levels; **sleep deprivation**, which disrupts normal neurotransmitter activity; and **mental health disorders** like schizophrenia and bipolar disorder, where dopamine dysregulation is a key factor. Additionally, **PTSD (Post-Traumatic Stress Disorder)** can cause chronic stress and trauma, leading to ongoing dopamine dysregulation and hallucinations. **Hypoxia**, or oxygen deprivation, sometimes seen during surgery or in critical conditions, can disrupt normal brain functions, including dopamine regulation, resulting in confusion and hallucinations. **Anesthesia and sedation** used during medical procedures can also temporarily alter dopamine levels and other neurotransmitters, causing post-surgical hallucinations as the brain reawakens from sedation.

These triggers can heighten the brain's sensitivity to internal thoughts, making them seem as though they are coming from an external source.

4. Miscommunication Between Language Centers:

The brain has specific areas that handle language—understanding words and creating speech. If something goes wrong in these areas, it can generate voices or speech even when no one is speaking. This miscommunication within the brain can lead to hearing what seems like external voices, even though they're being created entirely within our own minds.

The Role of Inner Desires and Fears

Manifestation of the Subconscious Mind

Our subconscious mind plays a significant role in how we process and understand the world around us, often influencing our thoughts and emotions without us even realizing it. Suppressed emotions and unresolved issues can sometimes surface as auditory experiences, including hearing voices. These voices can be a manifestation of deeply held desires, fears, or inner conflicts that have not been fully processed consciously.

For instance, someone experiencing intense guilt or anxiety may "hear" a voice that reflects their self-doubt or criticism, while someone with unfulfilled longings may perceive reassuring or affirming voices that seem to offer comfort. These auditory experiences are not external realities, but rather the mind's way of bringing to the surface emotions that have been pushed down or ignored. The brain creates these experiences as a means of processing complex feelings or unresolved psychological issues, using voices as a tangible way to address internal conflicts.

Coping Strategies

In some cases, hearing voices can serve as a protective mechanism during periods of emotional distress. When faced with overwhelming situations—such as intense grief, fear, or stress—the mind may generate voices as a way to provide relief or guidance. These voices often function as a coping strategy, helping individuals navigate their emotional turmoil. The mind, in its brilliance, can

48

create an auditory experience that feels like external advice or reassurance, which can offer comfort in moments of desperation.

One common manifestation of this is the "voice of God" phenomenon, where individuals believe they are hearing divine messages in the midst of crisis. For some, this perceived communication provides a sense of safety and direction, particularly when life feels uncertain or out of control. In these moments, the brain produces a "voice" that aligns with the individual's desire for protection, stability, or guidance. This allows the person to find a way out of a critical emotional moment, believing that the voice is offering divine support. While these voices can provide temporary comfort, they are, in many cases, the mind's way of coping with overwhelming stress rather than true external communication.

Anecdotal Evidence

From Christianity to Sikhism to New Age, anecdotes of hearing from the divine (however it is defined) are a dime a dozen on the internet.

Consider this one from Ashley Melillo on her website, *AshleyMelillo.com*:

> Divine messages.   Are you familiar with the idea?
>
> I find this particular topic is best introduced with a personal anecdote. With that in mind, **allow me to tell you a story about the day the Universe called me on my cell phone...**
>
> Flashback to November 1, 2019.
>
> This was at the peak of a time period where my husband

and I were making lots of big, life-changing decisions. Buying a home, career pivots, major financial changes, deciding whether or not we were ready to expand our family with another little one, etc.

The energy was high and my mind had been spinning with doubt and uncertainty for weeks on end.

In a moment of humbled decision fatigue that morning, I closed my eyes, placed my hands over my heart, and asked the Universe to please offer me a sign that the decisions we were making were in the best interest of our family.

"Universe, I'm here, I'm listening, I'm ready to be guided. If we're on the right path, please give me a clear sign."

Just a few hours later, this happened...

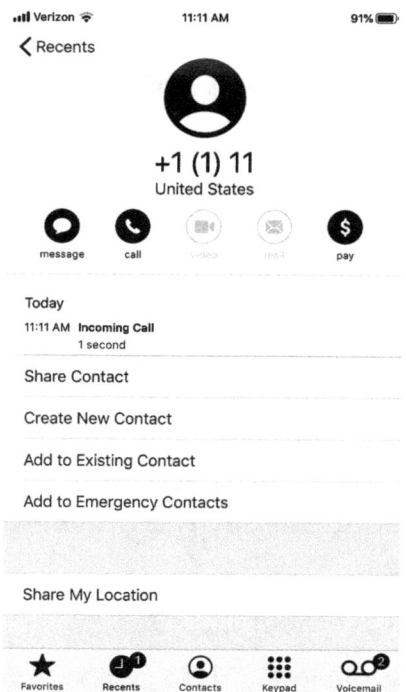

Randy White

On 11/1 at 11:11am the phone number 1 (1) 11 called me.

I answered—if the Universe calls, you'd best pick up—only to be gently hung up on 1 second later.

I immediately called the number back and received an error message from Verizon saying that the call couldn't be completed as dialed.

If this wasn't a divine message from the Universe, I don't know what would be. I'd asked for clear confirmation, and I'd received it in a divine (and modern) way.

In the weeks that followed, we proceeded forward with the decisions as we'd been planning, staying the course even in spite of several roadblocks that cropped up along the way.

With nearly a year of hindsight on our side, I can confidently say that the Universe was right.[2]

Incidentally, the call was most likely one of the following:

1. A scam attempt
2. A technical glitch in how the number was displayed on her phone
3. A spoofed number used to hide the call's true origin

Ashley's strong desire for a sign from the universe led her to interpret this call in a way that was meaningful to her, which brings us to our next topic.

---

2   Melillo, Ashley. "How to Hear Divine Messages." Ashley Melillo, 14 Oct. 2020, *https://www.ashleymelillo.com/blog/how-to-hear-divine-messages*. Accessed 20 Sept. 2024.

Confirmation Bias in Perceived Divine Communication

Understanding Confirmation Bias

Confirmation bias is the tendency for people to favor information or experiences that confirm their preexisting beliefs or expectations while disregarding or minimizing information that contradicts them. In essence, we are more likely to notice and interpret events in ways that reinforce what we already believe. This bias operates subconsciously and affects how we perceive and process information, particularly in areas where our emotions or deeply held beliefs are involved. When it comes to religious or spiritual experiences, confirmation bias can play a powerful role in shaping how individuals interpret their thoughts, feelings, and sensory experiences, including the perception of hearing divine voices.

Influence on Interpreting Voices

For individuals who believe in divine communication, confirmation bias can influence how they interpret auditory experiences, such as hearing voices. If a person already holds the belief that God communicates directly with them, they may be more likely to interpret internal thoughts, subconscious desires, or even random auditory hallucinations as external, divine messages. This tendency arises from the brain's desire to make sense of ambiguous experiences by aligning them with established beliefs.

For example, a person might hear a faint voice in a moment of stress or anxiety and, because of their existing belief that God speaks to them, interpret this voice as a divine

Randy White

message of guidance or reassurance. Instead of considering alternative explanations, such as the mind's natural coping mechanisms or misinterpreted internal thoughts, they attribute the experience to an external, supernatural source. In this way, confirmation bias serves to validate and strengthen their belief in personal divine communication, even if the experience is purely psychological.

Impact on Belief Systems

Once confirmation bias has influenced the interpretation of such experiences, it often becomes a self-reinforcing cycle. Each perceived divine message serves as "proof" that the individual is truly hearing from God, further entrenching their belief in personal revelation. Over time, this pattern of interpretation can lead individuals to place increasing trust in these subjective experiences, often at the expense of objective reasoning or external validation.

This cycle can lead to potential misguidance, as relying solely on subjective experiences leaves little room for critical examination. Instead of questioning whether the voice they "hear" aligns with biblical teachings or rational thought, individuals may become more convinced of the validity of these voices, further reinforcing their belief. In extreme cases, this reliance on subjective, emotionally charged experiences can lead to decisions that conflict with scriptural principles or reality, as the individual interprets every significant thought or sensation as divine guidance.

By understanding confirmation bias and its role in shaping perceptions, individuals can become more aware of how their beliefs may color their experiences. This awareness allows for a more balanced approach to interpreting spiritual or auditory experiences, emphasizing the importance of grounding faith in the teachings of Scripture rather than relying on fleeting, subjective sensations.

The Mind's Creation of Convincing Experiences

The Brilliance of the Human Mind

The human mind is an extraordinary organ, capable of creating vivid and deeply convincing internal experiences that often blur the line between imagination and reality. Whether through dreams, daydreams, or emotional responses, the brain has the ability to conjure sensations and experiences that feel entirely authentic, even when no external stimulus exists. This is particularly true in situations involving heightened emotions or stress, where the mind may generate internal dialogue, visualizations, or even auditory phenomena as a way of processing complex feelings or unresolved psychological tensions.

One of the ways the mind can convince us of the reality of these experiences is by drawing on deeply ingrained beliefs, memories, and desires. A person who is seeking direction in their life might subconsciously create a vivid auditory experience that feels like divine guidance. In this state, the distinction between what is real and what is imagined can become unclear. Because these internal experiences often feel so personal and immediate, the individual may interpret them as external and trustworthy. The power of the mind to create such convincing sensations reflects its brilliance, but it also highlights the potential for confusion between what is genuinely real and what is internally produced.

Randy White

Reinforcement Through Repetition and Recognition

Once these internal experiences occur, their frequency and recognition play a crucial role in reinforcing the belief that they are valid and genuine. The more often a person experiences an auditory phenomenon, such as hearing a voice they interpret as divine, the stronger their conviction that the experience is real. Repetition is a key factor here—just as practicing a skill makes it feel more natural, repeatedly experiencing what seems like divine communication can make it feel more believable. Over time, these internal experiences may solidify into a personal narrative of ongoing communication with a higher power.

Additionally, mental rehearsal and focused attention on these experiences can further strengthen their impact. A person who spends time reflecting on or seeking out these perceived messages may find that they become more frequent or more intense. In these cases, the brain's capacity to revisit and reinforce previous experiences makes the phenomenon even more convincing. The individual may become more attuned to these experiences, noticing subtle auditory cues or internal impressions that they previously would have ignored or dismissed.

The reinforcement of these experiences becomes even stronger when a person's church or spiritual community validates and endorses them. When fellow believers or spiritual leaders confirm the authenticity of these experiences as divine communication, the individual's confidence in their validity increases significantly. This external validation acts as a powerful form of social reinforcement, making it harder for the individual to question the experiences or consider alternative explanations. In many faith communities, such validation creates a feedback loop: the more the individual shares their experiences and receives confirmation from others, the more deeply rooted their belief in the divine origin of these experiences becomes.

Together, the repetition of these auditory experiences and the recognition from a supportive spiritual environment work to strengthen the conviction that these internal phenomena are not just psychological but truly divine. This combination of personal experience and external validation can create a powerful sense of certainty, making it difficult to critically examine or challenge the authenticity of these perceived communications.

Conclusion

Throughout this chapter, we have explored the psychological mechanisms that contribute to hearing voices and how these experiences, while sometimes startling, are a common part of human cognition. Stress, grief, fatigue, and intense desires can all trigger auditory phenomena, which the mind often generates as a way to cope with internal emotions and unresolved issues. These auditory experiences—ranging from internal dialogue mistaken for external voices to more vivid auditory hallucinations—are not inherently signs of mental illness. Instead, they represent the brilliance of the human mind's capacity to process and express deep-seated thoughts and feelings.

However, we have also seen how these experiences can be misinterpreted, particularly within a faith context. The normalcy of auditory experiences, combined with confirmation bias, can lead individuals to perceive these voices as divine communication. Left unchecked, this misattribution can result in a reinforcement cycle that strengthens one's belief in personal divine messages, especially when these experiences are validated by a supportive spiritual community.

While hearing voices can be a natural response to emotional or psychological triggers, these experiences should not automatically be equated with divine guidance. Instead, believers are encouraged to ground their faith in the sufficiency of Scripture, which provides a clear and objective standard for discerning God's communication. Personal experiences, no matter how convincing, should be evaluated critically in light of biblical teachings. This approach ensures that faith remains anchored in truth, rather than being swayed by fleeting and subjective experiences.

In the next chapter, we will explore how these psychological experiences can evolve into firm beliefs. We will discuss the progression from auditory experiences to deeply held convictions and the potential dangers of mistaking psychological phenomena for divine communication. As we continue, we will build on the foundations laid here, examining how belief systems are shaped and reinforced through both internal and external influences.

Randy White

CHAPTER 4:

The Progression from Psychological Experience to Belief

Throughout history, individuals have reported life-altering experiences—auditory, visual, or emotional—that they believe to be divine in nature. These experiences often become foundational to personal identity and spiritual life. In previous chapters, we examined the sufficiency of God's Word, the ways churches encourage hearing from God, and the psychological processes behind auditory hallucinations. In this chapter, we turn our attention to how these psychological phenomena evolve into entrenched beliefs.

We will explore how deeply emotional and mental experiences, especially those occurring in heightened states of stress or desire, can lead to vivid psychological manifestations that are misinterpreted as divine. Through the reinforcement of existing belief systems and communal affirmation, these experiences grow into powerful convictions, shaping not only personal faith but also behaviors and life decisions.

This chapter aims to dissect the cycle of belief reinforcement and examine its implications, demonstrating how normal psychological experiences can be magnified into spiritual significance. By drawing on historical examples, such as Joan of Arc's reported visions, we can further investigate how subjective psychological phenomena have shaped not only individual lives but entire historical movements. Joan's story serves as a key example of how a powerful inner conviction, interpreted as divine, can ignite a movement and how belief in one's spiritual mission, bolstered by communal affirmation, can turn psychological experiences into historical turning points.

The Reinforcement of Psychological Experiences Through Belief

The Cycle of Experience and Belief

The journey from experiencing an auditory phenomenon to firmly believing it is a message from God often follows a cyclical pattern. This cycle is fueled by psychological experiences that capture attention and are then interpreted through the lens of existing belief systems. Over time, this process reinforces the perception of these experiences as divine, making subsequent occurrences more readily accepted and deeply ingrained in one's faith.

Initial Psychological Experiences

As we've explored in previous chapters, stress, desire, and emotional states can lead to auditory experiences that feel remarkably real. These initial psychological events serve as the catalyst for a cycle that can profoundly impact an individual's belief system.

1. Stress and Emotional Turmoil

    Periods of intense stress or emotional upheaval often heighten our sensory perceptions and mental responsiveness. The mind, seeking equilibrium, may generate auditory experiences as a coping mechanism. For instance, someone facing a significant life challenge—such as job loss, relationship difficulties, or health concerns—might hear a reassuring voice offering guidance or comfort. This voice feels external but is, in reality, a manifestation of the mind's attempt to navigate through turmoil.

2. **Deep-Seated Desires and Longings**

   Intense desires can also precipitate auditory experiences. When an individual yearns for a particular outcome—a new opportunity, a relationship, or a sense of purpose—the mind may produce voices or prompts that align with these desires. For example, someone aspiring to embark on a missionary journey might "hear" a voice affirming this path, interpreting it as divine approval. The emotional investment in the desired outcome amplifies the significance of the experience.

3. **Capturing Attention and Prompting Reflection**

   These auditory experiences are impactful because they are unexpected and deeply personal. They capture the individual's attention, prompting reflection on their meaning and origin. The vividness of the experience, combined with its relevance to the person's current circumstances, makes it difficult to dismiss. This initial impact sets the stage for the experience to be interpreted within a broader belief framework.

Interpretation Through Belief Systems

Our beliefs act as lenses through which we interpret our experiences. For individuals within religious contexts, especially those that endorse the idea of personal divine communication, these lenses are finely tuned to perceive and ascribe spiritual significance to various phenomena.

1. **Framework of Existing Religious Beliefs**

   When an auditory experience occurs, the individual naturally seeks to understand it. If their faith tradition teaches that God speaks to believers personally, the experience is readily framed as divine communication. Scriptures, teachings, and testimonies within the community provide a backdrop that normalizes such occurrences. For instance, biblical accounts of God speaking to prophets or apostles reinforce the expectation that God can and does communicate directly with individuals today.

2. Ascribing Meaning to Ambiguous Stimuli

   Humans have an inherent tendency to find patterns and assign meaning to ambiguous stimuli—a psychological phenomenon known as apophenia. In the context of faith, this means that believers may interpret random or internally generated experiences as intentional messages from God. A fleeting thought, a coincidence, or an unexplained sound can take on profound significance when filtered through a spiritual lens.

   Consider a person who, after praying for guidance, hears a phrase or word that seems relevant to their situation. Even if the source is internal or simply random, their belief system primes them to accept it as an answer to prayer. This interpretation is further solidified if the experience aligns with their desires or resolves a dilemma they are facing.

3. Validation Through Scripture and Community

   The interpretation of these experiences is often reinforced by selectively referencing scriptures that support the idea of personal revelation. Passages that speak of God guiding, speaking, or revealing Himself to individuals are highlighted, while less emphasis is placed on scriptures that caution against relying on subjective experiences.

Randy White

Additionally, sharing these experiences within a faith community can lead to affirmation and encouragement. When others respond positively— perhaps sharing similar experiences or expressing belief in the validity of the encounter—it strengthens the individual's interpretation of the event as divine.

Reinforcement Loop

The cycle of experience and belief doesn't stop at a single occurrence; it becomes a self-reinforcing loop that deepens conviction over time.

1. Belief Strengthening Perception

    Once an individual accepts an experience as divine, their belief in personal communication from God is reinforced. This strengthened belief increases their attentiveness to future experiences, making them more likely to notice and interpret subsequent psychological events as divine messages. The mind becomes attuned to seeking and recognizing what it perceives as God's voice.

    For example, after interpreting a comforting voice during a stressful time as God's intervention, a person may become more vigilant for similar signs. Their heightened expectation makes them more susceptible to interpreting normal thoughts or feelings as divine communication.

2. Increased Frequency of Experiences

    The reinforcement loop can lead to an increased frequency of perceived divine messages. The individual's belief primes their mind to generate more of these experiences, especially during times of emotional intensity. Each new experience serves as additional "evidence" supporting their belief, creating a compounding effect.

3. Entrenchment of Conviction

   Over time, this cycle can entrench the conviction that they are regularly hearing from God. The belief becomes deeply integrated into their faith and identity, making it challenging to question or reassess. This entrenchment can have significant implications for decision-making, relationships, and overall well-being.

4. Resistance to Contradictory Evidence

   As the reinforcement loop solidifies the belief, individuals may become resistant to alternative explanations. Cognitive dissonance—the mental discomfort experienced when confronted with information that contradicts existing beliefs—leads them to dismiss or rationalize away conflicting evidence. This resistance further strengthens the cycle, as only confirming experiences are acknowledged.

Understanding this cycle is crucial for several reasons. **It highlights how easily normal psychological experiences can be misinterpreted as divine communication, especially within supportive religious frameworks**. It also underscores the importance of grounding one's faith in **objective truth** rather than **subjective experiences**, which, while compelling, can be misleading.

In the next section, we will delve deeper into the cognitive biases that facilitate this cycle, such as confirmation bias and the mechanisms of self-fulfilling prophecies. By examining these psychological factors, we can better appreciate the complexities involved in interpreting personal experiences and the potential risks of allowing them to supersede the authority of Scripture.

Randy White

Social and Community Validation

The reinforcement of psychological experiences as divine communication is not solely an internal process; it is significantly influenced by the social and communal contexts in which an individual operates. Religious communities and spiritual leaders play a pivotal role in validating and amplifying these experiences, thereby deepening personal convictions and shaping belief systems.

Role of Religious Communities

Religious communities serve as a social framework that can either question or reinforce an individual's interpretation of their experiences. When members share their perceived divine communications within these communities, the reactions and feedback they receive can greatly impact how they internalize and act upon these experiences.

1. Sharing Experiences and Collective Affirmation

   In many faith communities, sharing personal testimonies of hearing from God is not only encouraged but celebrated. Testimony sessions, prayer groups, and informal gatherings provide platforms for individuals to recount their experiences. When someone shares a story of divine communication, the community often responds with enthusiasm, support, and affirmation. This collective affirmation serves several functions:

   ◆ **Validation of the Experience:** Positive responses from others reinforce the individual's belief that their experience is genuine and significant.

   ◆ **Normalization:** Hearing others share similar experiences creates a sense of normalcy around the phenomenon, reducing doubts or fears about its legitimacy.

◆ **Encouragement to Seek More Experiences:** Community support can motivate individuals to remain open to future experiences, further embedding the cycle of experience and belief.

For example, a person who shares that they felt God leading them to a new job opportunity may receive congratulations and praise for their faithfulness in listening to God's voice. This reaction strengthens their conviction that they are indeed hearing from God and encourages others to seek similar guidance.

2. Impact on Personal Conviction

The communal validation of personal experiences has a profound impact on an individual's conviction. The support and reinforcement from trusted community members enhance the emotional and psychological significance of the experience. This can lead to:

◆ **Increased Confidence:** The individual feels more confident in their ability to discern God's voice, reducing self-doubt.

◆ **Strengthened Identity:** The experience becomes a defining aspect of their spiritual identity, influencing how they see themselves within the community.

◆ **Resistance to Contradictory Views:** Affirmation from the community can make the individual more resistant to questioning or reevaluating their experience, even in the face of conflicting evidence or perspectives.

Furthermore, the communal aspect can create a feedback loop where the individual's experiences inspire others,

Randy White

who in turn share their own experiences, reinforcing the collective belief in personal divine communication.

Authority Figures and Leadership

Spiritual leaders hold significant influence within religious communities. Their teachings, interpretations, and responses to congregants' experiences can greatly shape how individuals perceive and integrate their own experiences of hearing from God.

1. Influence of Pastors, Priests, and Spiritual Leaders

   Authority figures often serve as interpreters of spiritual experiences, providing guidance on how to understand and respond to perceived messages from God. Their influence manifests in several ways:

   ◆ **Teaching and Doctrine:** Leaders who preach about the importance and reality of personal divine communication set a theological foundation that supports and encourages such experiences.

   ◆ **Personal Counseling:** In one-on-one settings, leaders may affirm an individual's experiences, offering interpretations that align with the community's beliefs.

   ◆ **Public Recognition:** Acknowledging individuals who share their experiences in public forums can elevate the perceived importance and legitimacy of these encounters.

   For instance, a pastor who frequently shares anecdotes of God speaking to them may inspire congregants to seek similar experiences. When a church leader validates a member's testimony from the pulpit, it not only reinforces that individual's belief but also signals to the entire congregation that such experiences are desirable and credible.

2. Weight of Endorsements from Respected Figures

Endorsements from respected spiritual leaders carry significant weight due to their perceived authority and closeness to the divine. When these figures affirm an individual's experience, it can have the following effects:

- **Deepened Conviction:** The endorsement serves as powerful confirmation, making the individual more certain of the divine origin of their experience.

- **Influence on Others:** Other community members may also accept the validity of the experience based on the leader's endorsement, further reinforcing communal belief.

- **Reduced Critical Examination:** The authority's affirmation can discourage individuals from critically examining their experiences, as questioning may feel akin to doubting the leader or the faith itself.

Moreover, leaders who have their own experiences of hearing from God may model a pattern of behavior that congregants strive to emulate. This dynamic can create an environment where personal revelations are not only accepted but expected as a hallmark of genuine faith.

3. Potential Risks of Unquestioned Validation

While affirmation from community and leaders can strengthen faith, it also carries potential risks:

- **Suppression of Doubt:** Individuals may feel discouraged from expressing doubts or seeking alternative explanations for their experiences.

Randy White

◆ **Groupthink**: The desire for conformity within the community can lead to uncritical acceptance of experiences, even those that may be harmful or misleading.

◆ **Amplification of Extremes:** In some cases, unquestioned validation can lead individuals down paths that diverge from scriptural teachings or rational judgment, especially if the experiences encourage extreme actions.

For example, if a spiritual leader endorses a congregant's claim that God has called them to undertake a risky or unethical action without careful discernment, it can result in negative consequences for the individual and the community.

Digging Deeper:

The "Call" to Ministry and the Cycle of Affirmation

In many evangelical churches today, the concept of being "called" to ministry has taken on a deeply personal and often mystical dimension. This idea of a mysterious, inward call from God adds another layer to the cycle of affirmation and endorsement we discussed earlier. Pastors and ministry leaders are frequently encouraged to seek a divine confirmation of their calling, which can inadvertently lead them into the same patterns of seeking and interpreting psychological experiences as direct communication from God.

Albert Mohler, President of The Southern Baptist Theological Seminary, encapsulates this modern perspective:

> "Through His Spirit, God speaks to those persons He has called to serve as pastors and ministers of His church. The great Reformer Martin Luther described this inward call as 'God's voice heard by faith.' Those whom God has called know this call by a sense of leading, purpose, and growing commitment."[3]

While this view emphasizes a personal, spiritual experience of calling, it can contribute to the reinforcement loop where individuals interpret internal desires or thoughts as divine mandates. The expectation of a mystical call can place significant pressure on aspiring pastors to experience something extraordinary, potentially leading them to misconstrue normal psychological processes as supernatural confirmation.

The Shift from Church Call to Personal Call

Historically, the selection of church leaders was more communal and less centered on personal, subjective experiences. The early church often identified leaders based on observable qualities, doctrinal soundness, and the affirmation of the congregation. The Apostle Paul, in his pastoral epistles, provides guidelines that focus on character and ability rather than mystical experiences.

In **1 Timothy 3:1**, Paul states:

---

3   https://www.biblestudytools.com/bible-study/topical-studies/has-god-called-you-to-ministry.html)

Randy White

> "This is a true saying, If a man desire the office of a bishop, he desireth a good work."

Here, the emphasis is on the *desire* for the office—a noble aspiration—and not on receiving a special revelation or hearing an audible voice from God. The qualifications that follow in the subsequent verses focus on the candidate's character, conduct, and aptitude to teach, suggesting that these tangible attributes are the basis for recognizing a potential leader.

The Role of the Church in Recognizing Gifts

Rather than relying on a mysterious call, it is more biblically sound to return to a model where the church plays an active role in identifying and affirming those who are equipped for ministry. This approach involves:

- ▶ **Observing Gifts and Abilities:** The congregation and existing leadership can recognize individuals who demonstrate the necessary skills and spiritual maturity for pastoral roles.

- ▶ **Assessing Character and Doctrine:** Potential leaders can be evaluated based on their adherence to sound doctrine and the qualities outlined in Scripture.

- ▶ **Communal Affirmation:** The collective discernment of the church body can serve as confirmation of a person's suitability for ministry, reducing the pressure on individuals to seek personal revelations.

By adopting this model, the church can help prevent the cycle where pastors feel compelled to experience a mystical call. It acknowledges that the **Bible is sufficient** to equip believers for "every good work" (2 Timothy 3:16-17) and that God's guidance often comes through His Word and the wisdom of the faith community.

Navigating the Desire for Confirmation

For many aspiring pastors, the internal desire to serve can be strong and genuine. It's natural to seek confirmation that one's aspirations align with God's will. However, relying solely on subjective experiences can lead to the same pitfalls we've discussed:

- ▶ **Seeking Validation Through Experiences:** The expectation of a mystical call can lead to seeking out or fabricating experiences to meet communal or personal expectations.

- ▶ **Potential for Disillusionment:** If the anticipated experiences don't occur, individuals may doubt their suitability for ministry or their relationship with God.

- ▶ **Modeling The Mystical:** By insisting on a "call from God," churches and their pastors are modeling a mystical model rather than a sufficiency of Scripture model.

By shifting the focus from seeking mystical confirmations to embracing the sufficiency of Scripture and the discernment of the faith community, pastors and leaders can find a more stable foundation for their calling. This approach not only aligns with biblical teachings but also helps mitigate the risks associated with the cycle of psychological reinforcement and communal pressure.

Cognitive Biases and Self-Fulfilling Prophecies

As we delve deeper into the mechanisms that reinforce the belief in personal divine communication, we should examine the cognitive biases that underpin these processes. **Cognitive biases are systematic patterns of deviation from norm or rationality in judgment, which often influence our perceptions and decisions unconsciously**. Understanding these biases sheds light on how individuals may unknowingly reinforce their beliefs, sometimes at the expense of objectivity and truth.

Understanding Cognitive Biases

Cognitive biases play a crucial role in how we interpret experiences and information. They can lead us to favor information that confirms our existing beliefs and ignore or dismiss evidence that contradicts them. Two significant biases relevant to our discussion are **confirmation bias** and **attribution bias**.

Confirmation Bias
Definition and Explanation

Confirmation bias is the tendency to search for, interpret, and recall information in a way that confirms or supports one's prior beliefs or values. This bias leads individuals to give more weight to evidence that aligns with their existing convictions while disregarding or minimizing information that challenges them. It operates subconsciously, influencing how we gather and process information, and affects our ability to make objective decisions.

Examples of Confirmation Bias in Interpreting Experiences

In the context of believing that one hears from God, confirmation bias can significantly influence how individuals perceive and validate their experiences:

- **Selective Attention to Supporting Evidence:** A person may pay close attention to instances that seem to confirm that God is speaking to them, such as coincidental events, feelings of peace after making a decision, or scripture passages that appear to align with their thoughts. For example, if someone believes God wants them to take a particular job, they might focus on all the positive signs supporting that choice while ignoring any red flags or practical concerns.

- **Interpretation of Ambiguous Events:** Ambiguous or neutral events are often interpreted in a way that supports existing beliefs. If a person hears a song on the radio that mentions a theme relevant to their situation, they might see it as a divine sign, even though it could be a coincidence.

- **Memory Recall Favoring Beliefs:** Individuals may remember instances that support their belief in hearing from God more vividly than those that do not. Over time, this selective memory strengthens their conviction, as they recall numerous "confirmations" of God's communication.

Dismissal of Contradictory Evidence

Confirmation bias also involves the dismissal or rationalization of evidence that contradicts one's beliefs:

- **Ignoring Inconvenient Facts:** If outcomes do not align with the perceived divine guidance—such as a decision leading to unfavorable results—the individual may downplay these outcomes or attribute them to external factors like spiritual warfare or testing, rather than reconsidering their initial interpretation.

- **Rationalizing Discrepancies:** Contradictory experiences may be reinterpreted to fit the existing belief system. For instance, if a predicted event based on a perceived message from God does not occur, one might conclude that God changed His mind or that they misinterpreted the timing, rather than questioning the validity of the initial experience.

- **Discrediting Sources of Contradictory Information:** Information or feedback from others that challenges the belief may be dismissed by questioning the credibility or spiritual maturity of the source.

Impact on Belief Reinforcement

By filtering information in this biased manner, individuals create a self-reinforcing loop where their belief in personal divine communication becomes increasingly resistant to challenge. This loop strengthens their conviction but can also lead them further away from objective truth and, potentially, from the teachings of Scripture.

Attribution Bias
Definition and Explanation

Attribution bias refers to the systematic errors made when people evaluate or try to find reasons for their own and others' behaviors. It involves the tendency to attribute events to external factors, such as other people's actions or, in this context, divine intervention, rather than considering internal factors or coincidences.

Tendency to Attribute Events to External Forces

In the realm of faith and perceived divine communication, attribution bias manifests in several ways:

- **Externalizing Positive Outcomes:** Individuals may attribute favorable events or successes to God's direct intervention. For example, finding a parking spot close to the entrance may be seen as a blessing from God, reinforcing the belief that He is actively guiding their daily life.

- **Minimizing Personal Agency:** People might downplay their role in achieving goals or making decisions, instead crediting God for orchestrating events. While acknowledging God's sovereignty is a theological concept, overemphasis on this can diminish personal responsibility and critical thinking.

- **Interpreting Random Events as Signs:** Random or coincidental occurrences are often seen as deliberate messages or guidance from God. For instance, receiving a phone call from an old friend after praying about loneliness might be interpreted as a direct answer from God, even though it could be coincidental.

Examples in Personal Experiences

- **Misattributing Internal Thoughts:** An individual may perceive their own thoughts or ideas as coming from God rather than recognizing them as products of their own mind, especially if those thoughts align with their desires or fears.

♦ **Overemphasis on Symbolism:** Seeing symbolic meaning in everyday objects or events, such as a butterfly landing nearby being a sign of God's presence, reflects attribution bias. While such moments can be meaningful, overreliance on them for guidance can be misleading.

The Mechanism of Self-Fulfilling Prophecies

Understanding the mechanism of self-fulfilling prophecies is essential in comprehending how beliefs can shape reality, especially in the context of perceiving divine communication. A self-fulfilling prophecy occurs when a person's expectations about a situation or another person lead them to act in ways that cause those expectations to come true. In the realm of faith and personal experiences of hearing from God, this mechanism can significantly reinforce and solidify one's beliefs.

Expectation Influencing Perception

Our expectations have an amazing impact on how we perceive the world around us. When individuals hold strong beliefs or expectations, especially regarding spiritual matters, these beliefs can shape their sensory experiences and interpretations of events.

1. Shaping Sensory Experiences Through Belief

   The human brain is adept at filtering and interpreting sensory information based on prior knowledge, beliefs, and expectations. This phenomenon is evident in various psychological studies where participants perceive stimuli differently depending on what they expect to see or hear.

In the context of perceiving divine messages:

◆ **Heightened Sensitivity to Expected Stimuli:** If a person strongly believes that God communicates with them, they become more attuned to perceiving signs or messages in their environment. This heightened sensitivity means they may notice patterns, sounds, or events that others might overlook or consider insignificant.

◆ **Interpretation of Ambiguous Stimuli:** Ambiguous sounds or sights are more likely to be interpreted in line with one's expectations. For instance, a rustling of leaves might be perceived as a whispering voice, or a random sequence of numbers might be seen as a significant spiritual message.

◆ **The Role of Emotion:** Strong emotions tied to beliefs can intensify sensory experiences. During periods of intense prayer or worship, emotional arousal can make internal thoughts or feelings seem external, reinforcing the perception of divine communication.

2. The Psychological Process of Manifesting Expected Outcomes

The expectation of hearing from God can, in some cases, lead individuals to subconsciously create the experiences they anticipate. This process involves several psychological mechanisms:

◆ **Mental Priming:** Constant focus on the desire to hear from God primes the mind to generate experiences that align with this desire. The brain, seeking to fulfill the expectation, may produce thoughts, images, or sounds that are then perceived as external communications.

◆ **Mixing Up Inner Thoughts with Outside Messages:** Sometimes, people mistake their own thoughts and feelings for messages coming from God. This isn't done on purpose - it's like our brain gets a bit confused and can't tell the difference between what's happening inside our mind and what's coming from outside. It's similar to how you might think you heard someone call your name in a crowded place, but it was just your imagination.

◆ **Selective Memory and Attention:** Expectations influence what we pay attention to and remember. People are more likely to notice events that confirm their beliefs and recall them more vividly, reinforcing the expectation.

Example Scenario

Consider someone who is seeking guidance on an important life decision, such as choosing a career path. If they strongly expect God to provide direction:

◆ **Perception Influenced by Expectation:** They may interpret a casual comment from a friend, a billboard advertisement, or a song lyric as a divine sign pointing them toward a particular choice.

◆ **Internal Thoughts Externalized:** Their own subconscious leanings toward one option may manifest as an internal voice that they perceive as God's guidance.

◆ **Reinforcement of Belief:** Each perceived sign

strengthens their belief that God is communicating directly with them, making future similar experiences more likely.

Behavioral Reinforcement

The way individuals act on their perceptions further reinforces their beliefs. When actions are taken based on perceived divine messages, and especially when these actions lead to favorable outcomes, the belief in the authenticity of these messages is strengthened.

1. How People Act on Messages They Think Are from God

   When people believe God has spoken to them, they might:

   ◆ Make big life changes, like moving or switching jobs

   ◆ Start new habits, like praying more or giving to charity

   ◆ Tell others about their experience

2. How Results Affect Beliefs

   What happens after people act on these messages can strengthen their beliefs:

   ◆ Good results make people more sure the message was from God

   ◆ Bad results are often seen as tests or lessons from God

3. The Cycle of Expectation, Perception, and Action

   This process creates a self-reinforcing cycle:

   ◆ **Expectation Leads to Perception:** The belief that God will communicate causes individuals to interpret experiences as divine messages.

   ◆ **Perception Leads to Action:** Acting on these

perceived messages further ingrains the belief.

◆ **Action Influences Future Expectations:** Positive reinforcement from outcomes increases the expectation of future communications, making the individual more attuned to perceiving them.

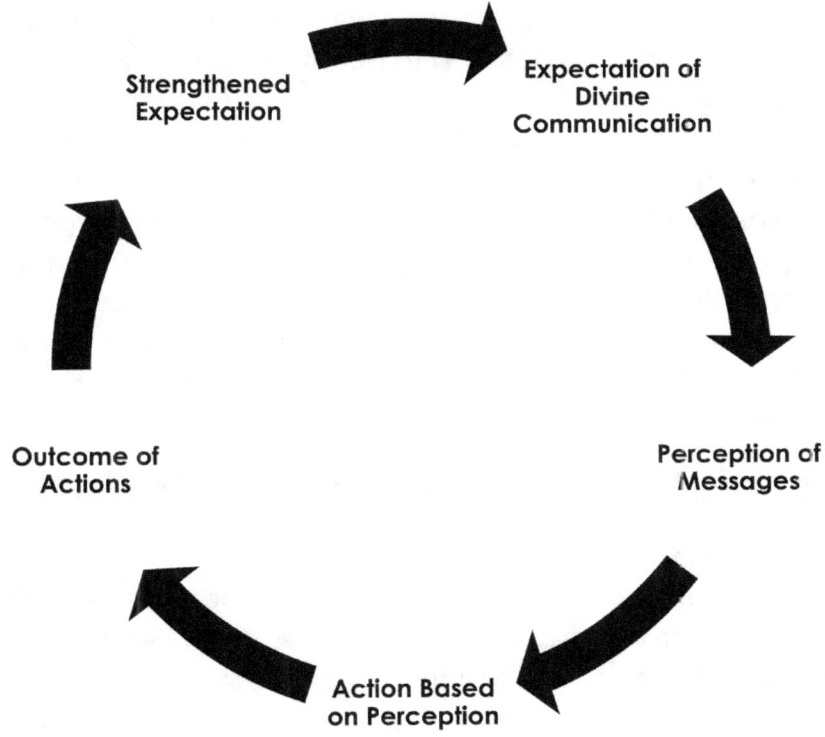

Example in a Church Setting

A congregant believes that God is calling them to start a new ministry. They act on this by organizing events and, when these events are well-received, they interpret the success as confirmation of God's guidance. Their actions and the positive outcomes reinforce their belief, leading them to expect and perceive further divine direction.

The Risks of Self-Fulfilling Prophecies

While the mechanism of self-fulfilling prophecies can reinforce positive behaviors and strengthen faith, it also carries potential risks. Decisions based solely on perceived messages may not always align with practical wisdom or scriptural principles, leading to negative consequences. Individuals may become overly confident in their ability to discern God's will, neglecting humility and the counsel of others. Reliance on subjective experiences can overshadow the importance of objective guidance from Scripture and sound reasoning. Furthermore, if outcomes repeatedly do not align with expectations, individuals may experience doubt, confusion, or a crisis of faith. These risks highlight the need for careful discernment and balanced interpretation of spiritual experiences.

Escalation to Deeper Conviction Through Action

As individuals continue to perceive voices or messages they believe are from God, these experiences often begin to influence their actions in significant ways. Acting on these perceived messages can deepen one's conviction and how this process can affect relationships and personal identity.

Acting on the Voices

Decision-Making Influenced by Perceived Divine Guidance

When people believe they are receiving direct communication from God, it naturally impacts their

Randy White

decision-making. They may start to make important life choices based on these perceived messages, trusting that they are following divine direction.

For example:

- **Career Choices:** Someone might feel led to change careers after "hearing" that they should pursue a different path. Believing that God is guiding them, they may leave a stable job to start a new venture that aligns with what they think is God's plan for them.

- **Relationships:** An individual might end or begin a relationship because they believe God has instructed them to do so. They trust that following this guidance will lead to better alignment with their spiritual journey.

- **Major Life Decisions:** Choices like moving to a new city, starting a ministry, or making significant financial investments can be influenced by these perceived messages. The belief that God is directing these decisions provides a strong sense of purpose and confidence.

These experiences often lead to successful or fulfilling outcomes, largely because those acting are responsible and godly individuals to begin with. The outcomes reinforce the individual's belief that they are indeed hearing from God.

Positive Feedback Loop

When actions taken based on perceived divine messages result in positive outcomes, it creates a reinforcing cycle:

1. **Perceived Divine Message:** The individual believes they have received guidance from God.

2. **Action Taken:** They act on this guidance, making

decisions or changes in their life.

3. **Positive Outcome:** The action leads to a favorable result, such as personal fulfillment, success, or improved relationships.

4. **Reinforced Belief:** The positive outcome strengthens their belief that they correctly heard and followed God's voice.

5. **Increased Reliance on Voices:** Encouraged by the results, they become more inclined to seek and trust these voices for future decisions.

This cycle can become self-perpetuating. Each successful outcome makes the individual more confident in their ability to discern and act on what they believe are divine messages. Over time, they may rely more heavily on these perceived communications when making decisions.

Intensification of Belief

As the positive feedback loop continues, the belief in personal communication with God can become deeply ingrained, affecting how individuals see themselves and interact with others.

Integration into Personal Identity

The conviction that one is hearing from God can become a central part of an individual's identity:

1. **Core Self-Concept:** They may view themselves as specially chosen or particularly attuned to God's will. This belief can provide a strong sense of purpose and significance.

2. **Resistance to Questioning:** Because this belief is tied to their self-identity, they may resist questioning or doubting the authenticity of the voices. Challenging

the messages might feel like challenging their relationship with God or their sense of self.

For example, someone might say, "I know God speaks to me; it's a fundamental part of who I am." This strong identification makes it difficult for them to consider alternative explanations for their experiences.

Isolation from Alternative Perspectives

As their belief intensifies, individuals may begin to distance themselves from those who do not share or support their convictions:

- **Avoiding Dissenting Opinions:** They might steer clear of conversations or relationships where their experiences could be questioned or critiqued. This avoidance helps them maintain their belief without facing conflicting viewpoints.

- **Potential Conflicts:** Differences in belief can lead to tension with friends, family, or community members. Loved ones who express concern may be seen as unsupportive or lacking faith, creating relational strain.

- **Creating Echo Chambers:** Surrounding themselves with only those who affirm their experiences can lead to a lack of balanced perspective. Without constructive feedback, they may become more entrenched in their beliefs.

Digging Into An Historical Example: Joan of Arc

Joan of Arc, also known as Jeanne d'Arc, was a French peasant girl who became a military leader and national hero during the Hundred Years' War between France and England. Born around 1412 in the village of Domrémy in northeastern France, she claimed to have experienced visions and heard voices from saints instructing her to support Charles VII and help expel the English from France.

Joan's Visions

Joan of Arc's visions are one of the most intriguing aspects of her life. Around the age of 13, she began to experience what she described as supernatural voices and visions. She claimed that these voices came from saints, particularly St. Michael, St. Catherine of Alexandria, and St. Margaret of Antioch. Joan said these saints appeared to her in physical form and gave her clear instructions to assist in liberating France from English domination and to see Charles VII crowned king.

- **St. Michael**, the archangel often depicted as a warrior leading the heavenly army, was the first to appear to her. He is traditionally associated with battles, so this might have shaped her understanding of the call to military action.

- **St. Catherine of Alexandria** and **St. Margaret of Antioch** were revered saints in medieval France, known for their virginity and martyrdom. Joan identified with these virtues, and the two saints became prominent voices guiding her decisions.

Joan said these visions came with the command that she was to lead an army to lift the siege of Orléans and ensure the coronation of Charles VII in the city of Reims. According to her testimonies, these visions were accompanied by bright lights, a strong sense of divine presence, and a conviction of her role in God's plan for France.

I chose Joan of Arc for this example because, while many evangelicals are comfortable with a person receiving a "word from God," almost all of them would be uncomfortable believing that Joan of Arc received visions from God through three Catholic saints. If we can prove that the history-changing "visions" of Joan of Arc can be seen from a viewpoint that rejects a supernatural interpretation, then we can also believe that our neighbor, family member, or even pastor who received a word from God, a still small voice, or a vision from God may also *feel deeply* that what they had was from God, but it can be interpreted in a different manner entirely.

The Nature of the Visions

Joan's visions were often described in terms of hearing "voices" rather than continuous visual experiences. She said that, at times, she would physically see the saints who spoke to her, but much of her guidance came from these internalized voices.

Interestingly, Joan was quite reluctant at first to reveal her visions to others. She feared being disbelieved or ridiculed, and her sense of their divine origin was deeply personal. However, as she gained confidence in the saints' instructions, she began to tell local leaders and eventually gained an audience with Charles VII. Her conviction in the reality of her visions was instrumental in convincing Charles to support her military endeavors.

Impact on Her Military Leadership

Joan's visions directly influenced her military strategy and tactics. She consistently claimed that her instructions came directly from God, mediated through the saints. This gave her extraordinary confidence, even in the face of overwhelming odds. The visions fueled her belief in the righteousness of her cause, which translated into the fierce loyalty of her troops and the rallying of French morale.

One of her most famous military achievements was the lifting of the siege of Orléans in 1429, which she accomplished after taking command of the French forces. Her visions gave her a strategic confidence that made her a formidable and inspirational figure, though she had no formal military training.

The Church's Changing Stance on Joan's Visions

Joan's claims of divine guidance were met with skepticism during her lifetime, culminating in her trial by an English-backed ecclesiastical court in 1431. The court accused her of heresy and witchcraft, asserting that her supposed divine revelations were demonic. Despite Joan's firm testimony, she was condemned to death and burned at the stake on May 30, 1431, at the age of 19. However, the Church's view of Joan's visions evolved over time. In 1456, the Catholic Church conducted a posthumous retrial, nullifying her conviction and declaring her a martyr. This shift in perspective culminated in Joan's canonization as a saint in 1920, with her visions now considered authentic and part of the spiritual legacy that established her as both a French hero and an inspirational figure in Christian history.

Skepticism and Interpretation

Joan of Arc's "visions" were pivotal not only to her personal sense of mission but also to the course of French history, altering the trajectory of the Hundred Years' War and contributing to the eventual French victory.

But could there be a different viewpoint?

Joan of Arc's story, especially her leadership at the Siege of Orléans, is often attributed to her claim of divine visions. However, an alternative analysis can view her "visions" as a powerful expression of her deep inner desire for French victory. This interpretation allows us to examine the psychological and social dynamics at play, rather than seeing her experiences strictly as supernatural.

Joan's Vision as a Manifestation of Inner Desire

Joan's claim to hear voices and see visions from St. Michael, St. Catherine, and St. Margaret can be reinterpreted as her own subconscious desires and convictions coming to the surface in a way that she, living in a deeply religious society, understood as divine communication. As a young peasant girl who witnessed the devastating effects of the Hundred Years' War and the occupation of her homeland, Joan might have developed an intense desire to see France liberated and its rightful king, Charles VII, crowned.

Joan's "visions" are actually psychological expressions of her inner drive and determination. Her mind, shaped by the religious environment of the time, expressed these desires in the form of saintly visitations. These visions provided Joan with a sense of mission and purpose, allowing her to articulate her inner passion in a form that would resonate not only with herself but also with those around her. This sense of certainty and divine endorsement gave her the psychological edge and self-confidence to approach the French court and present herself as God's chosen messenger for France's deliverance.

Passion and Leadership

Once Joan articulated this divine mission with conviction, it became contagious. The French forces, demoralized and fragmented, had been suffering from years of defeats and internal divisions. Many of their commanders were in a state of indecision, unwilling or unable to lead the kind of aggressive, decisive action needed to change the course of the war.

Joan's passion and confidence filled the leadership vacuum. Her boldness in declaring that God had sent her to liberate France and crown Charles VII imbued her with a charisma that transcended her social status and age. Her fervent belief in the righteousness of the cause, and her unwavering determination, became a rallying cry for the soldiers. In this sense, her conviction served as a form of psychological warfare, reinvigorating the troops and generating a shared sense of purpose, which is often termed esprit de corps.

Esprit de Corps: A Pseudo-Spiritual Force

Esprit de corps is a concept that describes the collective morale, unity, and dedication within a group, especially in a military context. Although it isn't spiritual in the religious sense, it can often take on a pseudo-spiritual quality in terms of the shared sense of higher purpose and emotional bonding among soldiers. Joan's passionate faith in her mission functioned as a catalyst for this kind of unifying force among the French troops.

Joan's arrival and the intense belief that she was divinely

Randy White

inspired stirred the French forces from their despondency. Her courage, combined with her declared divine backing, inspired the soldiers to fight not just for survival but for God, country, and king. This produced a transformative psychological shift, turning what had been a dispirited army into one capable of daring feats on the battlefield.

In the context of the Siege of Orléans, Joan's presence galvanized the French soldiers. They no longer saw themselves as fighting a losing battle but instead as instruments of God's will, led by a chosen leader who was bringing about a divinely-ordained victory. This shift in morale—from resignation to enthusiasm—was a decisive factor in the victory. The soldiers fought with renewed vigor, and Joan's boldness in leading from the front only amplified this spirit.

The Element of Surprise

The English forces, having dominated the French for years, likely did not anticipate the sudden resurgence of French morale and unity. From the English perspective, Joan might have seemed like an anomaly or a sideshow, and they may have underestimated her impact on the battlefield. The English had been entrenched in their positions around Orléans for several months, and they had been systematically defeating the French in various battles prior to Joan's arrival. Their overconfidence could have caused them to let down their guard.

When the French forces, spurred on by Joan's leadership and the newfound belief in their cause, launched a series of aggressive assaults on the English fortifications, they caught the English by surprise. The French, under Joan's banner, were not fighting with the same caution or hesitation that had characterized their earlier efforts. Instead, they attacked with boldness and intensity, traits that Joan had instilled in them through her relentless focus on the idea of victory ordained by God.

The English, who had likely expected the French to continue in their demoralized and divided state, were unprepared for the sudden shift in the battlefield dynamics. This unexpected vigor from the French troops, led by Joan, broke the English hold on Orléans and forced them to retreat.

Psychological Impact on the English

It's important to note that Joan's perceived divine backing did not only affect the French soldiers—it also played a role in demoralizing the English troops. Joan's reputation as a messenger from God spread rapidly. The English, who had previously been confident in their military superiority, now faced an army that believed itself to be on a divinely mandated mission. Such a belief in one's opponent can have a demoralizing effect, causing doubt and fear.

Joan's conviction that she was guided by God introduced an element of psychological warfare that transcended mere strategy. The English were no longer fighting just the French forces; they were fighting an army that believed it had divine protection and endorsement. For the English soldiers, the sudden shift in momentum and the unexpected ferocity of the French attacks may have contributed to a loss of morale, leading to their eventual retreat.

Randy White

CHAPTER 5

From Belief to Delusion

When does strong belief become delusion? This question lies at the heart of many spiritual and psychological journeys. While faith in unseen truths can provide strength and purpose, sometimes a grounded belief transforms into an unshakable conviction detached from reality and resistant to reason. At what point does fervent faith cross into delusional thinking, and how can we discern the difference?

Scripture intertwines belief and delusion with the acceptance or rejection of truth. The Apostle Paul warns in **2 Thessalonians 2:11–12**: "And for this cause God shall send them strong delusion, that they should believe a lie: That they all might be damned who believed not the truth, but had pleasure in unrighteousness." Paul addresses those who, after rejecting God's truth, are allowed to fall into deception because they have turned away from what is true.

Similarly, **Isaiah 44:20** describes the self-deception of idol worshippers: "He feedeth on ashes: a deceived heart hath turned him aside, that he cannot deliver his soul, nor say, Is there not a lie in my right hand?" This reflects those who cling to falsehoods, unable or unwilling to recognize the lies they have embraced.

These scriptures underscore a key biblical principle: when the mind strays from God's truth, it becomes vulnerable to delusion. This is often a consequence of willfully turning away from trusting in Scripture alone. The delusion is not merely psychological—it is a spiritual state tied to rejecting truth and embracing lies.

As we explore the line between belief and delusion, these scriptures guide our understanding. They remind us that the truth of God's Word must anchor our minds. When belief strays from this foundation and is driven by personal desires or unchecked experiences, it can lead to self-deception and ultimately, delusion.

Defining Delusion: A Psychological and Theological Perspective

A Psychological Definition of Delusion

In psychological terms, a delusion is a firmly held false or irrational belief maintained despite overwhelming evidence to the contrary. Delusions remain unshaken even when confronted with contradictory facts. Individuals experiencing delusions are convinced of their truth and often dismiss or defend against any challenge.

Key characteristics of delusion include:

1. **Unshakable Conviction:** The person clings to their belief with absolute certainty, regardless of how irrational it appears to others. For example, someone may believe they have a unique, divine mission without any objective basis.

2. **Resistance to Contrary Evidence:** Delusions resist reason and facts. When faced with contradictory evidence, the individual may dismiss or reinterpret it to fit their narrative.

3. **Disconnection from Reality:** Delusions create a break from reality, affecting relationships, decision-making,

and daily functioning as the delusion dominates thinking and behavior.

Delusion involves an inability or refusal to align one's belief with objective reality, trapping the individual in untruth.

Note that while this is a "self-imposed" psychological delusion, finding freedom from it is extremely difficult. There are also delusions stemming from mental illness beyond the scope of this discussion.

A Theological Perspective on Delusion

In theological terms, delusion results from rejecting God's truth and embracing falsehood, often due to willful disobedience. The Bible shows that turning away from truth opens people to deception; this rejection invites delusion to take hold.

Jeremiah 14:14 warns about false prophets who prophesy lies in God's name, following the deceit of their own hearts. These prophets believed they spoke for God but were deluded by their desires, spreading falsehoods and leading others astray.

Proverbs 1:24–31 illustrates that ignoring God's counsel leads to disaster: "Because I have called, and ye refused... Therefore shall they eat of the fruit of their own way." Rejecting wisdom leads to being consumed by one's own false beliefs, falling into delusion.

Biblical examples include King Saul (1 Samuel 28), who, after God ceased communicating with him due to disobedience, sought guidance from a medium, leading to further deception. Similarly, in 1 Kings 22, King Ahab is deceived by false prophets and a "lying spirit" as judgment for consistently rejecting God's truth.

Thus, delusion is a consequence of rejecting God's truth. Scripture warns that embracing lies leads to spiritual blindness, making individuals vulnerable to deception and ultimately, destruction.

Signs of Delusional Thinking

A critical distinction must be made between strong faith and delusion. **Faith** is rooted in trust in God's revealed truth in Scripture, believing in His promises and character even when challenged. It is anchored in the objective truth of God's Word.

Delusion, however, occurs when belief detaches from God's truth and focuses on subjective or false realities, often arising when personal desires, emotions, or experiences become the primary guide instead of His Word. Prioritizing subjective experience over Scripture risks delusional thinking.

Signs of Delusional Thinking:

1. **Obsession with Subjective Experiences:** Overfocus on personal revelations or "words from God" not grounded in Scripture, seeking experiences that affirm beliefs even when conflicting with biblical truth, elevating personal feelings over God's Word.

2. **Rejection of Correction or Dissenting Views:** Isolating from those who question experiences or beliefs, viewing dissent as opposition to God's will rather than a call to reevaluate, refusing wise counsel (Proverbs 12:15).

3. **Overreliance on Internal Feelings:** Emphasizing feelings as evidence of God's leading, allowing emotions to become the primary authority rather than Scripture, making it difficult to discern between personal desires and God's will (Jeremiah 17:9).

In summary, strong faith remains grounded in Scripture and open to correction to align with God's Word. Delusional thinking focuses on personal experience, rejects correction, and relies too heavily on feelings, leading away from truth.

How Delusion Shapes Spiritual Life

Delusion Alters How One Reads Scripture

When belief becomes delusion, individuals often twist Scripture to fit their false narratives. They isolate verses, using selective interpretations to justify personal experiences or beliefs that contradict the Bible's broader teachings. Instead of approaching Scripture with humility to understand God's truth, they seek confirmation of their preconceived notions, treating Scripture as a tool to validate their subjective experiences.

This distortion manifests in various ways: focusing on prosperity promises while ignoring teachings on suffering, or latching onto vague prophecies to justify erratic behavior. False prophets in Jeremiah 14:14 prophesied lies, following the deceit of their hearts, twisting truth to support their delusions. Similarly, modern individuals may cherry-pick verses that seem to affirm their experiences, ignoring the fuller context that challenges them.

Even Satan used Scripture out of context when tempting Jesus (Matthew 4:5–7), reminding us how easily Scripture can be misused. True faith submits every experience to the authority of the whole counsel of God's Word; delusion bends Scripture to fit personal desires.

The Role of Pride in Delusion

Pride plays a pivotal role in the development and persistence of delusion. Delusional individuals often believe they have special insight or a unique connection with God, convincing themselves they are above correction or questioning. This spiritual pride blinds them to their errors and reinforces their delusion by making them resistant to truth.

Proverbs 16:18 warns, "Pride goes before destruction, and a haughty spirit before a fall." Believing oneself uniquely chosen or possessing higher spiritual insight leads to dismissing mature believers, pastors, or Scripture when it challenges their delusions. They may view dissenting voices as lacking faith or spiritually inferior.

This pride creates spiritual elitism, isolating individuals from the community that could offer wisdom and guidance. It feeds delusion by insulating them in a self-affirming bubble where beliefs are never questioned. Proverbs 29:1 states, "He who is often reproved, yet stiffens his neck, will suddenly be broken beyond healing." A heart hardened by pride refuses correction until severe consequences occur.

Breaking the Feedback Loop

Breaking free from delusion requires a humble effort to re-engage with Scripture, seek accountability among believers who rightly handle the word of truth (2 Timothy 2:15), and embrace humility in returning to truth.

* **Re-engaging with Scripture:** Deliberately return to Scripture, allowing the Bible to challenge and reshape beliefs. Reading the Bible in context, along with regular, prayerful study brings clarity and correction, helping realign with God's truth (**Hebrews 4:12**).

- **Accountability in the Church:** Isolation fosters delusion; re-engaging with biblical community is crucial. Seek wise counsel and accountability from mature Christians who can offer correction and guidance (**Proverbs 11:14**). Surrounding oneself with godly mentors and fellow believers helps break the cycle of self-affirmation and provides necessary checks on personal beliefs. *(Note: Choose a local church carefully due to prevalent theological errors.)*

True humility acknowledges human fallibility and the need for God's guidance. Recognizing our need for correction opens us to God's truth, allowing the deluded person to see their error and return to the church community for support and restoration.

The Spiritual Consequences: When the Mind Overpowers Scripture

A dangerous consequence of delusion is allowing personal experiences—visions, voices, impressions—to dominate over Scriptural truth. When subjective experiences are elevated above God's Word, it leads to self-deception. Historical examples, like Montanus, who claimed direct revelation from the Holy Spirit and formed a cult, caution us about prioritizing personal revelations over biblical truth.

Human emotions and inner impressions are unreliable guides, misleading people into believing they follow God's direction when acting on personal desires or fears. Allowing the heart to dictate faith risks being led astray.

Chapter 5

This shift from faith grounded in Scripture to one dominated by personal feelings is gradual but dangerous. A balanced faith remains anchored in God's Word. Prioritizing emotional highs or inner impressions as divine revelation leads to spiritual confusion, blurring lines between genuine faith and delusion, causing loss of sight of Scripture's objective truth.

Are You Delusional? Warning Signs for the Believer

Delusional thinking can subtly infiltrate a believer's life, often disguised as strong faith or spiritual insight. While Scripture should be our foundation, warning signs emerge when personal revelations overpower biblical truth. Key indicators that delusional thinking may be creeping in:

1. **You claim to trust Scripture but become upset when others question additional "words from God."** Becoming defensive when someone doubts your claimed revelations suggests reliance on personal experiences over biblical authority.

2. **You constantly seek signs or special messages from God.** Always looking for new divine signs instead of relying on Scripture overlooks the sufficiency of God's Word.

3. **You find yourself increasingly isolated from those closest to you.** Relationships become strained or hostile as focus on personal revelations grows.

4. **You miss opportunities for fellowship with family and friends.** Avoiding loved ones due to tension cuts you off from support and community.

Randy White

5. **You miss career or personal development opportunities.** Prioritizing personal revelations over practical responsibilities leads to neglect of growth opportunities.

6. **You see yourself as God's special agent with a unique message.** This belief elevates you above others, feeding spiritual pride.

7. **When others question your revelations, you accuse them of disrespect.** Feeling insulted when questioned indicates unwillingness to consider others' concerns.

These warning signs suggest drifting from Scripture and healthy fellowship. If you recognize these in your life, it's time to reassess, re-anchor in God's Word, and seek guidance from mature believers.

If several of these describe you now, consider seeking pastoral care you trust. Tell them, "I think I've accepted things as coming from God that were more related to my [wishful thinking/trauma/experiences] than to the Word of God. These have captivated my thinking and behavior, and I'm ready to begin putting my life back together."

You'll likely be amazed how quickly life returns to normal and how God's Word becomes a personal treasure once again.

Randy White

CHAPTER 6:

The Isolation and Breakdown of Relationships

David was the kind of man many admired—young, ambitious, and successful. He built a fast-growing business, had recently married, and seemed to have it all. A natural "go-getter," David thrived on high pressure and knew how to turn stress into motivation. But when a sudden tragedy struck, everything changed. An accident left his child on the brink of life and death, and David's world collapsed under the weight of grief and uncertainty.

In the face of this crushing burden, David did what many believers do: he turned to the Lord for strength. Seeking comfort, he became convinced that God had spoken to him directly about his son's life. He prayed fervently, sang over his child, and insisted that no one speak anything but faith. He rebuked any expression of doubt, angry at anyone who dared suggest an outcome other than full healing. But despite his faith and efforts, the boy succumbed to his injuries.

The loss devastated David. What followed was a period of overwhelming grief, marked by isolation and attempts to numb the pain. Marijuana and alcohol became coping mechanisms, anything to dull the emotional turmoil. But in his desperation, David once again heard what he believed was the voice of God. This voice, however, didn't bring him peace; it led him down a path of delusion. David abandoned reason, his business, and even his family and friends. He began wandering the country, hitchhiking and visiting places where he believed God was sending him to deliver prophetic warnings. He claimed to speak on behalf of God, denouncing sins, predicting disasters, and issuing judgments.

By the end, David's life was a tangled mess—spiritually, psychologically, and relationally. His firm belief that he was hearing directly from God had led him far from reality, leaving a wake of broken relationships and lost purpose. The problem was not just the tragedy he experienced, but how his understanding of God's communication through personal revelation opened the door to delusion. In a moment of stress and vulnerability, David experienced what is common to many: an auditory hallucination triggered by his emotional and psychological state. But his theological framework, which placed personal experience above Scripture, allowed this momentary experience to spiral into a life of confusion and disorder.

This chapter will explore how we can help future "Davids" before they fall into such delusion. Through a biblical lens, we will examine the dangers of placing personal revelation over the authority of Scripture and the consequences it can have on relationships, mental health, and spiritual life. By understanding the connection between stress, delusion, and isolation, we can intervene and provide guidance to those at risk, ensuring that they remain grounded in truth and supported by the community of faith.

Defining Delusion in a Biblical Context

Delusion, both spiritual and psychological, has its roots in a disconnect from truth. In the Bible, spiritual delusion is often the result of rejecting God's truth, which leads

Randy White

to a darkened understanding and a distorted view of reality. Romans 1:21-22 provides a clear example of this: *"Because that, when they knew God, they glorified him not as God, neither were thankful; but became vain in their imaginations, and their foolish heart was darkened. Professing themselves to be wise, they became fools."*

In this passage, Paul explains how those who knew of God's reality, rejected Him nonetheless, leading to a state of vanity and delusion. By turning away from the truth of God, they became trapped in their own reasoning, which, though they perceived it as wisdom, was in fact folly. This rejection of divine truth resulted in a darkened heart, a mind that could no longer perceive reality accurately. Here, we see a clear parallel to the psychological concept of delusion: a fixed, false belief that resists correction, even in the face of clear evidence. Spiritually, this manifests as an unwavering belief in something that opposes God's revealed Word, leading to a state of spiritual blindness.

Jeremiah 17:9 warns us of the inherent danger within the human heart: *"The heart is deceitful above all things, and desperately wicked: who can know it?"* This scripture reminds us that delusion is not just an external influence but can also arise from the deep deceit within our own hearts. When individuals trust in their own hearts and desires, especially in moments of vulnerability, they become more susceptible to delusion. Rather than relying on the truth of God's Word, they elevate their own feelings or experiences, which can lead them astray.

This type of delusion is not limited to mental health but involves a spiritual dynamic. Spiritual delusion occurs when individuals reject God's truth in favor of their own understanding, isolating themselves from both truth and community. Just as psychological delusion isolates a person from reality, spiritual delusion alienates them from God's reality, causing them to become disconnected from the life-giving truth found in Scripture. Over time, this not only affects their relationship with God but also severs meaningful connections with others as their beliefs become increasingly detached from reality.

In this way, both spiritual and psychological delusions share a common outcome: isolation from truth and community. Whether through a refusal to acknowledge reality or a rejection of God's Word, delusion creates barriers that leave individuals trapped in their own false beliefs, unable to receive correction or wisdom from outside sources. As believers, recognizing these warning signs is crucial in helping those caught in the cycle of delusion before they drift too far from truth.

Example: The Delusion of Earning Salvation Through Works

A person might believe that by doing good deeds, attending church, or being morally upright, they can secure favor with God and earn their way into heaven. This delusion is reinforced by emotions of self-righteousness and personal experiences of accomplishment, leading them to feel spiritually "safe" based on their own efforts.

However, Scripture is clear that salvation is by grace through faith, not by works. Ephesians 2:8-9 states: *"For by grace are ye saved through faith; and that not of yourselves: it is the gift of God: Not of works, lest any man should boast."* Trusting in good deeds or religious efforts rather than trusting in the finished work of Christ on the cross is a form of spiritual delusion. It is a belief that is resistant to correction, despite the clear teaching of Scripture.

Randy White

This delusion can cause individuals to believe they are spiritually secure when, in reality, they are relying on their own efforts, which can never bring salvation. If these individuals would trust the clear teaching of Scripture—that salvation comes through faith in Christ alone and not through works—they would escape this delusion and come to a true understanding of grace. This is an example where trusting experience, feelings of moral accomplishment, or personal interpretations leads to spiritual delusion, but trusting in the authority of Scripture leads to clarity and truth.

The Impact of Delusion on Personal Relationships

Delusion, especially spiritual delusion, does not merely affect an individual's thoughts and beliefs; it also has far-reaching consequences on their relationships. Scripture provides clear warnings about the dangers of self-deception and the relational breakdown that often accompanies it. Proverbs 12:15 says, *"The way of a fool is right in his own eyes: but he that hearkeneth unto counsel is wise."* This verse captures the essence of how delusional thinking can cause a person to stubbornly cling to their own beliefs, even when those beliefs are flawed or harmful. In contrast, wisdom is characterized by a willingness to listen to advice and accept correction.

When someone falls into spiritual delusion, they often reject the counsel of others, believing that they have unique spiritual insight that others lack. This rejection of correction can quickly lead to isolation. Proverbs 18:1 describes this process: *Through desire a man, having separated himself, seeketh and intermeddleth with all wisdom.*" In other words, a person caught in delusion tends to isolate themselves, following their own desires while rejecting the wisdom of those around them.

1. Rejecting Correction

One of the key marks of spiritual delusion is a refusal to accept correction. When an individual is convinced that they are receiving special revelation from God or have deeper spiritual understanding than others, they may view any attempt to correct them as an attack on their faith. Rather than considering the possibility that they could be wrong, they become defensive, refusing to listen to family, friends, or spiritual mentors. This rejection of advice is often accompanied by a sense of superiority—believing that others are not as spiritually mature or that they simply "don't understand."

The deluded individual may perceive any challenge to their beliefs as opposition, viewing those who attempt to offer wisdom as lacking in faith or being spiritually blind. Proverbs 12:15 emphasizes that wisdom involves the humility to accept counsel, but spiritual delusion leads to an inflated sense of self-righteousness and a closed mind.

2. Distancing from Loved Ones

As delusion takes deeper root, the individual begins to distance themselves from loved ones. Relationships with family and friends become strained as the person increasingly sees themselves as spiritually superior or as having a direct line to God that others cannot access. This leads to a breakdown in communication, where the deluded individual becomes unwilling to engage in meaningful conversations with those who question or challenge their beliefs.

Randy White

This isolation is not only relational but also spiritual. By cutting themselves off from the wisdom and counsel of others, the individual becomes more entrenched in their delusion, convinced that their path is right even as they spiral further into isolation. Proverbs 18:1 warns that this separation is driven by self-centered desire—seeking one's own way at the expense of sound wisdom. The more isolated a person becomes, the harder it is for them to break free from their delusional thinking because they lack the external voices that could offer correction and perspective.

3. Believing in Unique Spiritual Insight

A hallmark of spiritual delusion is the belief that the individual has received unique or special spiritual insight that others do not possess. This belief can cause them to view themselves as spiritually elite or chosen, which further alienates them from others. They may begin to distrust those who question their experiences or beliefs, labeling them as doubters or lacking in faith. This attitude creates a barrier between the deluded individual and those around them, deepening their isolation.

Over time, the individual may create a personal echo chamber where they only engage with people or ideas that affirm their delusion. This not only damages their relationships but also reinforces their belief that they are on the right path. As they continue to avoid wise counsel and reject differing perspectives, their delusion grows stronger, and their relationships continue to deteriorate.

The Role of Community and Accountability in Spiritual Health

In order to safeguard against spiritual delusion, churches, small groups, and families must make a crucial shift away from the prevalent "How to hear from God" mentality. Many denominations, in their eagerness to encourage personal spiritual experiences, have inadvertently fostered a culture where subjective impressions, emotions, or personal revelations are celebrated and elevated over the clear teaching of Scripture. This mindset, while often well-intentioned, opens the door to the very delusion this book seeks to address.

Instead of continuing to celebrate and validate every claim of personal revelation, it is vital for churches to return to the foundational belief that God's Word is fully sufficient. Proverbs 11:14 reminds us, *"Where no counsel is, the people fall: but in the multitude of counselors there is safety."* The most reliable "counselor" is the Bible itself. A firm commitment to the belief that the 66 books of the Bible represent the complete extent of God's communication to humanity can prevent many of the problems outlined in this book. By teaching the sufficiency of Scripture, we ground believers in unchanging truth, rather than in the instability of subjective experience.

1. Shifting Focus to "What Does the Bible Say?"

Churches should move away from teaching methods that emphasize "hearing from God" outside of Scripture. Rather than focusing on personal experiences, the focus should shift to the question, *"What does the Bible say?"* Encouraging congregants to turn to Scripture for guidance, rather than relying on fleeting impressions or emotional experiences, builds a strong foundation of truth and provides a reliable safeguard against delusion.

By fostering a culture of biblical literacy, where members are encouraged to study the Bible both literally and contextually, churches can help individuals rightly divide the Word of God. This involves teaching congregants to carefully apply biblical principles in the appropriate context, avoiding the common error of misapplying Scripture to fit personal desires or situations. When people understand Scripture properly, they are less likely to rely on their own subjective interpretations or experiences, thus reducing the risk of falling into spiritual delusion.

2. Teaching the Sufficiency of Scripture

The heart of this shift is a strong, consistent emphasis on the sufficiency of Scripture. 2 Timothy 3:16-17 declares that Scripture is "profitable for doctrine, for reproof, for correction, for instruction in righteousness: That the man of God may be perfect, thoroughly furnished unto all good works." This passage underlines that everything needed for life and godliness is found within the pages of the Bible. Churches must teach that the Bible, as God's final and complete revelation, contains all the guidance believers need. The pursuit of personal revelations outside of Scripture should be discouraged, as it often leads to confusion and distraction from the clear teachings of God's Word.

A commitment to the sufficiency of Scripture also means teaching that God's communication is closed—His revelation has been fully delivered within the 66 books of the Bible. Any claim to extra-biblical revelation, whether through dreams, voices, or personal impressions, must be seen as unnecessary, and potentially harmful, to the believer's spiritual health. By grounding people in the truth that God's Word is complete, believers are protected from the instability and uncertainty that comes from relying on subjective experiences.

3. Practical Steps for Churches to Implement a "Bible-First" Culture

Churches, small groups, and families can create environments where Scripture is honored as the sole authority for guidance and decision-making. Here are several practical ways to implement this Bible-first culture:

- **Prioritize Expository Preaching and Teaching:** Preaching should focus on carefully walking through passages of Scripture, explaining their meaning in context and applying them appropriately. This approach not only teaches the sufficiency of Scripture but also models how to study the Bible properly.

- **Discourage Overemphasis on Subjective Experiences:** While personal experiences can be meaningful, they should never be elevated above the authority of Scripture. Leaders should gently redirect conversations about hearing from God to what the Bible teaches. If someone shares a personal experience, they should be encouraged to evaluate it in light of Scripture, ensuring it aligns with God's revealed Word.

- **Promote Bible Study and Discipleship:** Encourage church members to engage in regular Bible study that prioritizes literal and contextual interpretation. Discipleship programs that focus on teaching how to rightly divide the Word of God will help congregants build a strong, personal relationship with Scripture rather than relying on personal revelations or mystical experiences.

- **Establish a Clear Doctrinal Position on the Sufficiency of Scripture:** Churches and denominations should adopt or reaffirm a clear doctrinal stance that God's communication to humanity is fully contained within the Bible. This doctrine should be emphasized from the pulpit, in Bible studies, and in small group settings. When the sufficiency of Scripture is firmly taught and believed, believers are less likely to seek spiritual insight outside of God's Word.

- **Encourage a Humble Approach to Scripture:** Remind congregants that understanding Scripture requires humility and community. Just as Proverbs 11:14 says there is safety in the multitude of counselors, studying Scripture together can help avoid misinterpretation. Believers should be encouraged to consult with trusted pastors or mentors when applying biblical principles, ensuring they are correctly handling the Word of truth (2 Timothy 2:15).

4. The Benefits of a Bible-Centered Community

When churches prioritize the sufficiency of Scripture, they create a culture where believers can grow in maturity and truth, without the confusion and instability that comes from subjective revelations. This Bible-centered approach fosters unity and spiritual health. Relationships within the church are strengthened as people hold one another accountable to God's Word, rather than to personal experiences.

By placing the Bible at the center of teaching, decision-making, and spiritual growth, churches can effectively prevent the kind of delusion that leads to isolation, relational breakdown, and spiritual confusion. In doing so, the entire community is built up in love, strengthened in truth, and safeguarded from the errors that come from placing personal experience above the clear authority of Scripture.

Building a Bible-First Culture

For churches and denominations to effectively combat the rise of spiritual delusion, they must make a firm commitment to teaching the sufficiency of Scripture. By shifting away from a "hearing from God" mentality and encouraging believers to ask *What does the Bible say?* churches can ground their members in truth and protect them from the instability of subjective experience. A Bible-first culture, built on the conviction that God's Word is complete and authoritative, offers the safety and wisdom that comes from a multitude of biblical counselors. Through this commitment, churches can help believers avoid the pitfalls of spiritual delusion and foster true spiritual health and growth.

Warning to Pastors and Bible Teachers

Pastors and Bible teachers have an important responsibility to guide their congregations in truth, carefully instructing them in sound doctrine. However, in today's church landscape, many teachers are tempted to prioritize emotional experiences and subjective revelations over the foundational truths of Scripture. This temptation is not a new one. Paul warned about it in 2 Timothy 4:3-4: *"For the time will come when they will not endure sound doctrine; but after their own lusts shall they heap to themselves teachers, having itching ears; and they shall turn away their ears from the truth, and shall be turned unto fables."*

This warning is clear: when leaders neglect sound teaching, they not only risk leading themselves astray but also endanger their congregation. Pastors and Bible teachers must be vigilant in ensuring that their instruction is rooted in the sufficiency of Scripture, not in subjective experiences or the pursuit of ongoing revelation. Failure to do so can foster an environment of delusional thinking, where believers begin to prioritize personal feelings and supposed "words from God" over the clear and reliable truth of the Bible.

1. The Danger of Teaching Ongoing Revelation

When pastors and teachers emphasize ongoing revelation—that God is constantly speaking to believers outside of Scripture—they unintentionally open the door to confusion and spiritual instability. This approach encourages members of the congregation to seek divine messages through personal experiences, impressions, or inner feelings, rather than turning to the Bible for guidance. While this can be exciting or emotionally satisfying, it ultimately fosters a mindset where subjective experiences are given greater authority than the unchanging Word of God.

The danger here is that personal revelations, while often sincere, are fallible and prone to error. Without the corrective standard of Scripture, individuals may interpret their own desires, fears, or imaginations as divine communication. This can lead to spiritual delusion, where believers become convinced they are hearing directly from God, even when their beliefs contradict biblical truth. By encouraging an emphasis on hearing from God outside of Scripture, pastors risk leading their congregations into the very error Paul warned against—turning away from the truth and embracing "fables" (2 Timothy 4:4).

2. The Call to Faithfulness in Scripture

To avoid these dangers, pastors and Bible teachers must remain faithful to the sufficiency of Scripture, as outlined in 2 Timothy 3:16-17: *"All scripture is given by inspiration of God, and is profitable for doctrine, for reproof, for correction, for instruction in righteousness: That the man of God may be perfect, thoroughly furnished unto all good works."* This passage, which we have relied upon throughout this book, emphasizes that Scripture contains everything necessary for teaching, correction, and spiritual maturity. God has provided His full and complete revelation in the Bible, equipping believers for every aspect of life and godliness.

Pastors and teachers must therefore resist the urge to supplement Scripture with personal revelations or emotional experiences. Instead, they should encourage their congregations to turn to the Bible as their ultimate authority, teaching them to seek God's will through careful study of His Word. By grounding their teaching in the clear truths of Scripture, pastors can protect their congregations

Randy White

from the confusion and instability that comes from relying on subjective experiences.

3. Avoiding a Culture of Subjectivity

Pastors must also be mindful of the culture they cultivate within their churches. If subjective experiences are celebrated or validated without discernment, it creates an environment where personal revelations are elevated to the same level as Scripture. This can lead to a dangerous precedent, where congregants feel pressured to "hear from God" in extraordinary ways or to rely on their emotions for spiritual guidance. In this type of culture, biblical truth can quickly take a backseat to individual interpretations and experiences.

To combat this, pastors should intentionally foster a culture that values sound biblical teaching above all else. Rather than encouraging personal revelations, pastors should model and promote a "Bible-first" mentality, where decisions, spiritual insights, and life choices are all filtered through the lens of Scripture. In doing so, they can help their congregations remain grounded in the unchanging truth of God's Word, rather than being swayed by the shifting winds of personal experiences or emotions.

Conclusion: The Call to Humility and Truth

Spiritual delusion is a subtle and dangerous trap, one that can isolate individuals from the truth of Scripture, their community, and even from a proper understanding of their relationship with God. Throughout this chapter, we have seen how delusional thinking not only distorts one's perception of truth but also damages personal relationships and hinders spiritual growth. Whether caused by a misplaced reliance on subjective experiences or an overconfidence in personal insight, spiritual delusion pulls individuals away from the grounding anchor of God's Word.

The antidote to delusion is a humble and steadfast commitment to biblical truth. Humility is essential for every believer, as it opens us to correction, community, and accountability. As Proverbs 11:14 reminds us, there is safety in a multitude of counselors. No believer is immune to error, and it is only through a posture of humility that we can grow in wisdom and avoid the pitfalls of self-deception. Recognizing our need for one another, we must remain willing to receive correction, guidance, and support from trusted spiritual mentors and fellow believers.

Ultimately, the call is to remain grounded in the sufficiency of Scripture. God's Word provides the wisdom and guidance we need for every area of life, and it alone must be our final authority in discerning truth from delusion. As 2 Timothy 3:16-17 teaches, Scripture is sufficient for doctrine, correction, and instruction in righteousness. When we place the Bible at the center of our spiritual lives—rather than subjective experiences or emotions—we safeguard ourselves from the confusion and instability that often accompanies spiritual delusion.

Let this be a call to humility and truth. Each of us, no matter our level of spiritual maturity, needs the correction and protection that comes from living within the bounds of biblical truth and healthy relationships. By remaining steadfast in Scripture and committed to godly community, we can navigate the challenges of faith with clarity, avoiding the dangerous drift into delusion. God's Word is sufficient, and in it, we find the firm foundation upon which to build a life grounded in truth.

Randy White

appendix a:

Divine Communication In Other Faiths

Throughout history, various religions have embraced the concept of divine communication, where believers perceive messages or guidance from a higher power. This appendix explores how different faiths understand and experience communication with the divine.

Islam

In Islam, divine communication is primarily conveyed through the Qur'an, which Muslims believe is the literal word of God (*Allah*) as revealed to the Prophet Muhammad through the angel Gabriel. Muslims also consider the Hadith—records of the Prophet's sayings and actions—as important guidance. While direct revelation is believed to have ceased with Muhammad, personal experiences like dreams or feelings may be interpreted as signs from Allah, but they are always evaluated against the teachings of the Qur'an and Hadith.

Judaism

Judaism holds that God communicated with prophets in the Hebrew Bible (*Tanakh*), conveying laws and teachings to guide the people of Israel. While the era of prophets is considered closed, prayer and the study of sacred texts are central to maintaining a relationship with God. Some Jewish traditions, especially in mysticism (*Kabbalah*), explore deeper spiritual experiences, but divine communication is generally understood through communal worship and adherence to the Torah.

Hinduism

Hinduism encompasses a wide range of beliefs and practices regarding divine communication. Many Hindus believe that the divine can be experienced directly through meditation, prayer, and rituals. Sacred texts like the Vedas and the Bhagavad Gita are considered revelations from the divine. Personal experiences of the divine, such as visions or insights during meditation, are valued and often sought after as a means of spiritual growth.

Buddhism

While Buddhism does not center on a creator deity, communication with transcendent truths is a key aspect of the faith. Enlightenment (Nirvana) is achieved through deep meditation and insight into the nature of reality. Some Buddhist traditions involve the invocation of bodhisattvas or celestial Buddhas for guidance. Revelatory experiences are personal and serve as milestones on the path to enlightenment.

Sikhism

Sikhism teaches that God communicates with humanity through the Guru Granth Sahib, the Sikh holy scripture, which is considered the living Guru. Sikhs believe in a personal relationship with the divine, cultivated through prayer, meditation on God's name (Naam Japna), and living a life of truth and service. Divine guidance is sought within the teachings of the Gurus as recorded in their scriptures.

Randy White

Indigenous Religions

Many Indigenous cultures around the world have rich traditions of divine communication. Shamans or spiritual leaders often serve as intermediaries between the spiritual and physical worlds. Communication with ancestors, spirits, or deities may occur through rituals, dreams, visions, or trance states, providing guidance for individuals and the community.

New Age and Contemporary Spirituality

New Age movements and contemporary spiritual practices often emphasize personal experiences of the divine. Practices such as channeling, meditation, and energy work are believed to facilitate communication with higher consciousness, spiritual guides, or universal energies. These experiences are highly individualized and may draw from multiple religious and philosophical traditions.

Baha'i Faith

The Baha'i Faith recognizes divine communication through a line of messengers from God, including Abraham, Moses, Buddha, Jesus, Muhammad, and most recently, Bahá'u'lláh. Baha'is believe that God's will is revealed progressively through these messengers. Personal prayer and meditation are means for individuals to draw closer to God and seek guidance, always in harmony with the teachings of Bahá'u'lláh.

Shinto

In Shinto, the traditional religion of Japan, communication with kami (spirits or deities) is integral. Rituals at shrines, offerings, and festivals are ways to honor the kami and seek their favor or guidance. While not centered on scripture, Shinto practices foster a connection with the divine present in nature and ancestral spirits.

Conclusion

Across diverse religions, the belief in divine communication reflects a fundamental human desire to connect with a higher power. While the methods and understandings vary—ranging from sacred texts and prophets to personal meditation and communal rituals— these practices underscore the importance of seeking guidance, meaning, and connection beyond the material world.

appendix B

Divine Communication Rejected By Evangelicals

Within the broader Christian tradition, numerous claims of divine communication have emerged that are not universally accepted. Evangelical Christians, who emphasize the authority of Scripture and the necessity of personal faith in Jesus Christ, often reject certain visions and revelations accepted by other Christian groups. This appendix explores some notable examples of such claims.

Marian Apparitions

Our Lady of Guadalupe

In 1531, a Mexican peasant named Juan Diego claimed that the Virgin Mary appeared to him on Tepeyac Hill near Mexico City. The apparition, known as Our Lady of Guadalupe, requested that a church be built on the site. As a sign, an image of Mary was miraculously imprinted on Juan Diego's cloak. This event is deeply significant in Roman Catholicism, symbolizing Mary's role in evangelization.

Evangelical Perspective: Evangelicals generally view such Marian apparitions with skepticism. They emphasize that Scripture does not support the veneration of Mary in this way and caution against experiences that might detract from the sole mediatorship of Christ (1 Timothy 2:5). The reliance on extra-biblical revelations is seen as leading believers away from the foundational truths of the Bible.

Visions of Saints and Angels
Apparitions of Saintly Figures

Throughout history, there have been numerous reports of saints and angels appearing to individuals, offering guidance, comfort, or warnings. For example, Saint Padre Pio, a Catholic priest, claimed to have regular visions and even bore the stigmata, the wounds of Christ.

Evangelical Perspective: Evangelicals typically reject these accounts as valid, and would mot often attribute them to psychological phenomena. They affirm that while God used angels in the past, such apparitions are not in the current experience of the believer. Experiences that elevate human figures or introduce new teachings are approached with doubt.

The Book of Mormon
Joseph Smith's Revelations

In the 19th century, Joseph Smith claimed to receive visions from God the Father and Jesus Christ, leading to the founding of the Church of Jesus Christ of Latter-day Saints (Mormonism). He asserted that an angel named Moroni guided him to golden plates containing the Book of Mormon, another testament of Jesus Christ.

Evangelical Perspective: Evangelicals reject the Book of Mormon and Joseph Smith's revelations, holding that the canon of Scripture is closed and sufficient. They contend that additional scriptures introduce doctrines inconsistent with the Bible. Revelation 22:18–19 is often cited, warning against adding to or taking away from God's revealed Word.

Modern Prophetic Movements

The New Apostolic Reformation (NAR)

In recent decades, movements like the NAR have emphasized modern-day apostles and prophets who claim fresh revelations from God. They advocate for a restoration of the apostolic offices and often predict future events or provide specific directives to the church.

Evangelical Perspective: While recognizing the ongoing work of the Holy Spirit, many evangelicals are wary of movements that place new revelations on par with Scripture. They stress the sufficiency of the Bible for teaching and guidance (2 Timothy 3:16–17) and caution against teachings that cannot be substantiated by Scripture.

Charismatic Experiences Emphasizing Extrabiblical Revelation

Heaven Tourism Books and Accounts

Books like "*Heaven is for Real*" recount personal experiences of visiting heaven or hell, often providing detailed descriptions and insights not found in Scripture.

Evangelical Perspective: Evangelicals often express skepticism toward such accounts, emphasizing that while God can work in mysterious ways, experiences must not supersede biblical revelation. They encourage discernment and prioritize Scripture over personal testimonies.

The Apocrypha and Deuterocanonical Books

Additional Biblical Texts

Certain Christian traditions, like Roman Catholicism and Eastern Orthodoxy, include additional books in their versions of the Old Testament, known as the Apocrypha or Deuterocanonical books.

Evangelical Perspective: Evangelicals typically do not accept these books as inspired Scripture, holding to the 66-book canon. They argue that these texts do not meet the criteria established for canonicity and that they were not recognized as authoritative by the Jewish community from which the Old Testament emerged.

Conclusion

Evangelicals place a strong emphasis on the authority and sufficiency of the Bible as God's revealed Word. Claims of divine communication that introduce new doctrines, elevate traditions, or cannot be substantiated by Scripture are generally rejected. This approach seeks to guard against teachings that might lead believers away from the core truths of the Christian faith as understood within evangelical theology.

By evaluating such claims through the lens of Scripture, evangelicals aim to remain faithful to what they believe is the authentic message of Christianity, ensuring that personal experiences or external teachings do not overshadow the foundational gospel of Jesus Christ.

Objections

- **Objection:** I don't believe that God is speaking to mankind as in additional Scripture-the canon of Scripture is closed-but, I think God may be speaking to some people individually for a personal circumstance, and not something that is applicable to mankind at large.

  ▷ **Response:** The Bible gives sufficient wisdom for all personal circumstances. Either the Bible makes the believer "perfect, throughly furnished unto all good works" (2 Tim. 3:17) or it does not!

- **Objection:** God is the same yesterday, today, and tomorrow. Therefore, if he spoke then, then why would he not speak today?

  ▷ **Response:** Wouldn't this require that God would speak in the same manner as He previously spoke? Even Hebrews 1:1-2 says that God has changed the manner of speaking to the world. If God is always operating the same way, then we should expect handwriting on the wall, burning bushes, and choirs of angels, at least from time to time, right?

- **Objection:** Didn't Jesus say that His sheep hear His voice (John 10:27)?

  ▷ **Response:** Biblically speaking, "His sheep" is Israel. Yet Israel is in a time of national spiritual blindness today. God will certainly call Israel to Him

- **Objection:** What about the Holy Spirit's leading and prompting?
  - ▷ **Response:** The concepts of "prompting" or "leading" of the Spirit are as vague and subjective as the "still small voice." Since these experiences are too subtle to verify, they should be regarded as mere feelings. Instead, rely on the Word of God as your sole source of authority.

- **Objection:** I've had a personal experience that was absolutely real and revealed God's will. Is this not legitimate?
  - ▷ **Response:** I have no doubt that your experience was real. However, I question your interpretation of that experience. Whether you heard a voice, felt a prompting, had a dream, or sensed God's presence strongly—was it truly a voice from God? These experiences are common to all people, regardless of their religious background. While these experiences are genuine, and following such "words" often leads to positive outcomes, I believe you experienced a psychological phenomenon that you're attributing to God's voice.

- **Objection:** Doesn't the Bible say we are to be led by the Spirit (Romans 8:14)?
  - ▷ **Response:** Romans 8:14 should be understood in light of verses like 2 Timothy 3:16-17, which states, "All scripture is given by inspiration of God, and is profitable for doctrine, for reproof, for correction, for instruction in righteousness: That the man of God may be perfect, thoroughly furnished unto all good works." This passage teaches that Scripture is

Randy White

sufficient for all spiritual guidance and good works. Additionally, Psalm 119:105 declares, "Thy word is a lamp unto my feet, and a light unto my path," emphasizing that God's written Word is the primary means of guidance for believers. To be led by the Spirit, in the context of Romans 8:14, is to "mortify the deeds of the body" (Rom. 8:13).

Randy White

About the Author

Dr. Randy White on the Sea of Galilee

Dr. Randy White is a theologian, author, and pastor with a lifelong commitment to teaching the Word of God and helping believers learn to "rightly divide the word of truth" (2 Tim. 2:15). Known for his unwavering dedication to the authority and sufficiency of Scripture, Dr. White challenges popular yet unbiblical doctrines with clarity, precision, and deep reverence for God's Word.

With decades of pastoral ministry experience, Dr. White has become a trusted voice in dispensational theology and biblical interpretation. His verse-by-verse teaching style, anchored in the inerrancy of Scripture and a literal reading of the Bible, has garnered an international audience through his ministry, **Randy White Ministries**. He is the author of multiple books that address critical theological issues and offer practical insights for living a biblically grounded life.

Dr. White holds a passion for exposing the dangers of modern mysticism and guiding believers back to the truth of God's Word. His teaching ministry equips Christians to question assumptions, reject unscriptural traditions, and embrace the sufficiency of the Bible for all matters of faith and practice.

When not teaching or writing, Dr. White enjoys the natural beauty of the Rocky Mountains, where he resides with his family. He continues to broadcast, write, and challenge believers to stand firmly on the unshakable foundation of Scripture.

Dispensational Publishing House is striving to become the go-to source for Bible-based materials from the dispensational perspective.

Our goal is to provide high-quality doctrinal and worldview resources that make dispensational theology accessible to people at all levels of understanding.

Visit our blog regularly to read informative articles from both known and new writers.

And please let us know how we can better serve you.

Dispensational Publishing House, Inc.
PO Box 3181
Taos, NM 87571

Call us toll free 844-321-4202

www.DispensationalPublishing.com

www.ingramcontent.com/pod-product-compliance
Lightning Source LLC
Chambersburg PA
CBHW070751120626
46557CB00002B/541